The Nursery Rhymes O[illegible]gland...

James Orchard Halliwell-Phillipps, Percy Society

PREFACE.

In the present age of literary revivals of all kinds, the members of the Percy Society will not perhaps reject an attempt to rescue from the hand of oblivion and introduce into notice the works of an ancient series of bards, who amidst the general resuscitation of early literature have never hitherto been favoured with any vindicating critic. That their works have at one time or other been in every one's mouth, is, I presume, a sufficient proof of their genuine right to fame; and if the names of their several authors be as difficult to settle satisfactorily, as that of the *Iliad* itself, yet the modesty that was the reason in the first instance of their being withheld, only serves now to enhance the reputation of these writers. The lullabies of the ancients are for ever lost, and a future race may not despise the knowledge of our method of primary instruction for our children, οτε παππαζουσι και μαμμαζουσι.

If we had any credible sources of information, it would be a subject worthy of investigation, to ascertain the origin of the popularity of these national nursery melodies: but, like most other branches of popular literature and traditional anecdotes, their history is wrapped up in great obscurity. We can ascertain that they have been current in our nurseries for nearly two centuries, in all parts of England, under forms very slightly differing from each other; but more than this we know not. And these traditional nonsense-scraps have come down to us in such numbers, that in the short space of three years the Editor of the present volume had collected considerably more than a thousand. A selection is here presented to the reader.

A few nursery rhymes can be traced back to a very early period. Every child will remember the lines on Bryan O'Lin,—

> "Bryan O'Lin, and his wife, and wife's mother,
> All went over a bridge together:

> The bridge was loose, and they all tumbled in,
> 'What a precious concern!' cried Bryan O'Lin:"

which are found, under a very slightly modified form, in a little black-letter book, by W. Wager, called, "*The longer thou livest the more Foole thou art*," printed about the year 1560:

> "Tom a Lin, and his wife, and his wives mother,
> They went over a bridge all three together;
> The bridge was broken and they fell in,
> The devil go with all, quoth Tom a Lin."

A few more examples of this kind will be found in the following pages.

In attempting a classification, I am well aware that much question may arise concerning the true appropriation of many of the nursery rhymes to their several classes, and I must claim the indulgence of my readers for any mistakes I have committed in this respect.

I may here also take the opportunity of stating, that it was originally my intention to have introduced also a collection of merriments upon which many of these rhymes are founded, but the project was overruled by a gentleman, who gave it as his opinion that the Society would by their publication be involved in an awkward question of copyright. I was not previously aware that "Goody Two Shoes," and romances of this kind, were regarded so jealously by the trade.

My respectful and grateful thanks are due to Sir Edward F. Bromhead, Bart. who most kindly and liberally furnished me with a very large and valuable collection of nursery rhymes from Lincolnshire, together with several useful suggestions, to which I have been greatly indebted.* Nor must I omit to mention my obligations to my friend Mr. Black, a member of the Council of the Percy Society, who has also kindly given me his valuable assistance.

J. O. H.

35, *Alfred Place*,
Feast of All Saints, 1841.

---

* I am in possession of a curious and clever satirical pamphlet, entitled "Infant Institutes," 8vo. Lond. 1797, to which I am indebted for some interesting scraps.

NURSERY RHYMES.

First Class.—Historical.

I.

WHEN good king Arthur ruled this land,
He was a goodly king;
He stole three pecks of barley-meal,
To make a bag-pudding.

A bag-pudding the king did make,
And stuff'd it well with plums:
And in it put great lumps of fat,
As big as my two thumbs.

The king and queen did eat thereof,
And noblemen beside;
And what they could not eat that night,
The queen next morning fried.

II.

[The following song, relating to Robin Hood, the celebrated outlaw, is well known at Worksop, in Derbyshire, where it constitutes one of the nursery series.]

Robin Hood, Robin Hood
Is in the mickle wood!
Little John, Little John,
He to the town is gone.

Robin Hood, Robin Hood
  Is telling his beads,
All in the green wood,
  Among the green weeds.

Little John, Little John,
  If he comes no more,
Robin Hood, Robin Hood,
  He will fret full sore!

III.

[The original of "The house that Jack built" is presumed to be a hymn in *Sepher Haggadah*, fol. 23, a translation of which is here given. The historical interpretation was first given by P. N. Leberecht, at Leipsic in 1731, and is printed in the "Christian Reformer," vol. xvii. p. 28. The original is in the Chaldee language, and it may be mentioned that a very fine Hebrew manuscript of the fable, with illuminations, is in the possession of George Offor, Esq. of Hackney.]

---

1. *A kid, a kid,* my father bought
For two pieces of money:
A kid, a kid.

2. Then came *the cat,* and ate the kid
That my father bought
For two pieces of money:
A kid, a kid.

3. Then came *the dog* and bit the cat,
That ate the kid,
That my father bought
For two pieces of money:
A kid, a kid.

4. Then came *the staff,* and beat the dog,
That bit the cat,
That ate the kid,
That my father bought
For two pieces of money:
A kid, a kid.

5. Then came *the fire,* and burned the staff,
That beat the dog,
That bit the cat,
That ate the kid,
That my father bought
For two pieces of money:
A kid, a kid.

6. Then came the *water* and quenched the fire,
That burned the staff,
That beat the dog,
That bit the cat,
That ate the kid,
That my father bought
For two pieces of money:
A kid, a kid.

7. Then came *the ox*, and drank the water,
That quenched the fire,
That burned the staff,
That beat the dog,
That bit the cat,
That ate the kid,
That my father bought
For two pieces of money:
A kid, a kid.

8. Then came *the butcher* and slew the ox,
That drank the water,
That quenched the fire,
That burned the staff,
That beat the dog,
That bit the cat,
That ate the kid,
That my father bought
For two pieces of money:
A kid, a kid.

9. Then came *the angel of death* and killed the butcher,
That slew the ox,
That drank the water,
That quenched the fire,
That burned the staff,
That beat the dog,
That bit the cat,
That ate the kid,
That my father bought
For two pieces of money:
A kid, a kid.

10. Then came the *Holy One,* blessed be He!
And killed the angel of death,
That killed the butcher,
That slew the ox,
That drank the water,
That quenched the fire,
That burned the staff,
That beat the dog,
That bit the cat,
That ate the kid,
That my father bought
For two pieces of money:
A kid, a kid.

The following is the interpretation:

I. The kid, which was one of the pure animals, denotes the Hebrews.

The father, by whom it was purchased, is Jehovah, who represents himself as sustaining this relation to the Hebrew nation. The two pieces of money signify Moses and Aaron, through whose mediation the Hebrews were brought out of Egypt.

2. The cat denotes the Assyrians, by whom the ten tribes were carried into captivity.

3. The dog is symbolical of the Babylonians.

4. The staff signifies the Persians.

5. The fire indicates the Grecian empire under Alexander the Great.

6. The water betokens the Roman, or the fourth of the great monarchies to whose dominion the Jews were subjected.

7. The ox is a symbol of the Saracens, who subdued Palestine, and brought it under the caliphate.

8. The butcher that killed the ox, denotes the crusaders, by whom the Holy Land was wrested out of the hands of the Saracens.

9. The angel of death signifies the Turkish power, by which the land of Palestine was taken from the Franks, and to which it is still subject.

10. The commencement of the tenth stanza, is designed to show that God will take signal vengeance on the Turks, immediately after whose overthrow the Jews are to be restored to their own land, and live under the government of their long-expected Messiah.

IV.

[The following version of a popular rhyme is in one of Douce's books. I consider it to refer to the rebellious times of Richard II.]

My father he died, I cannot tell how,
But he left me six horses to drive out my plough:
With a wimmy lo! wommy lo! Jack Straw blazey boys!
Wimmy lo! Wommy lo! Wob, wob, wob!

V.

My father he died, but I can't tell you how,
He left me six horses to drive in my plough:
With my wing wang waddle oh,
Jack sing saddle oh,
Blowsey boys bubble oh,
Under the broom.

I sold my six horses and I bought me a cow,
I'd fain have made a fortune, but did not know how:
With my, &c.

I sold my cow, and I bought me a calf;
I'd fain have made a fortune, but lost the best half:
With my, &c.

I sold my calf, and I bought me a cat;
A pretty thing she was, in my corner sat:
With my, &c.

I sold my cat, and I bought me a mouse;
He carried fire in his tail, and burnt down my house.
With my, &c.

VI.

[The same song as the preceding, dictated by a lady now living in the Isle of Man, but a far better version.]

MY daddy is dead, but I can't tell you how;
But he left me six horses to follow the plough:
With my whim wham waddle ho!
Strim stram straddle ho!
Bubble ho! pretty boy,
Over the brow.

I sold my six horses to buy me a cow,
And wasn't that a pretty thing to follow the plough?
With my, &c.

I sold my cow to buy me a calf,
For I never made a bargain, but I lost the best half.
With my, &c.

I sold my calf to buy me a cat,
To sit down before the fire, to warm her little back:
With my, &c.

I sold my cat to buy me a mouse,
But she took fire in her tail, and so burnt up my house:
With my, &c.

VII.

[There is an old proverb which says that "a cat may look at a king." Whether the same adage applies equally to a female sovereign, and is referred to in the following nursery song, or whether it alludes to the glorious Queen Bess, is now a matter of uncertainty.]

Pussy cat, pussy cat, where have you been?
I've been to London to see the Queen.
Pussy cat, pussy cat, what did you there?
I frighten'd a little mouse under the chair.

VIII.

The rose is red, the grass is green,
Serve Queen Bess our noble queen!
    Kitty the spinner
    Will sit down to dinner,
And eat the leg of a frog:
    All good people
    Look over the steeple,
And see the cat play with the dog.

IX.

[Taken from MS. Douce, 357, fol. 124. See Echard's *History of England*, book iii. chap. 1.]

SEE saw, sack-a-day;
Monmouth is a pretie boy,
  Richmond is another,
Grafton is my onely joy,
And why should I these three destroy,
  To please a pious brother?

X.

[Written in 1641, on the occasion of the marriage of Mary, the eldest daughter of Charles I, with the young Prince of Orange.]

WHAT is the rhyme for *porringer?*
The king he had a daughter fair,
And gave the Prince of Orange her.

XI.

[The following nursery song alludes to William III, and George, Prince of Denmark.]

WILLIAM and Mary, George and Anne,
Four such children had never a man:
They turn'd their father out of door,
And call'd their brother the son of a whore.

XII.

OVER the water, over the lee,
Over the water to Charley.
Charley loves good ale and wine,
Charley loves good brandy,
Charley loves a little girl,
As sweet as sugar-candy.

XIII.

[The following may possibly allude to King George and the Pretender.]

JIM and George were two great Lords,
They fought all in a churn;
And when that Jim got George by the nose,
Then George began to gern.

XIV.

POOR old Robinson Crusoe!
Poor old Robinson Crusoe!
They made him a coat,
Of an old nanny goat,
I wonder how they could do so!
With a ring a ting tang,
And a ring a ting tang,
Poor old Robinson Crusoe!

XV.

The king of France went up the hill,
  With twenty thousand men;
The King of France came down the hill,
  And ne'er went up again.

Second Class.—Tales.

XVI.

THERE was an old woman had three sons,
Jerry, and James, and John:
Jerry was hung, James was drowned,
John was lost and never was found,
And there was an end of her three sons,
Jerry, and James, and John!

XVII.

THERE was a man in Thessaly,
  And he was wondrous wise,
He jump'd into a quickset hedge.
  And scratch'd out both his eyes;
And when he saw his eyes were out,
  And he was in great pain,
He jump'd into a holly bush,
  And scratch'd 'em in again.

XVIII.

When I was a bachelor, I lived by myself,
And all the bread and cheese I laid upon the shelf;
The rats and the mice they made such a strife,
I was forced to go to London to buy me a wife;
The roads were so bad, and the lanes were so narrow,
I was forced to bring my wife home in a wheelbarrow.
The wheelbarrow broke, and my wife had a fall;
Deuce take the wheelbarrow, wife, and all.

XIX.

Rowsty dowt, my fire 's all out,
My little dame is not at home!
I'll saddle my cock and bridle my hen,
And fetch my little dame home again!
Home she came, tritty trot,
She asked for the furmety she left in the pot;
Some she eat and some she shod,
And some she gave to the truckler's dog;
She took up the ladle and knocked its head,
And now poor Dapsy dog is dead!

XX

ROBIN and Richard
Were two pretty men;
They laid in bed
Till the clock struck ten;
Then up starts Robin
And looks at the sky,
Oh! brother Richard,
The sun 's very high.
You go before with the bottle and bag,
And I will come after on little Jack Nag.
You go first, and open the gate,
And I'll come after, and break your pate.

XXI.

[From MS. Bib. Reg. 8 A. v. fol. 52, of the time of Henry VIII.]

WE make no spare
Of John Hunkes' mare;
And now I
Think she will die:
He thought it good
To put her in the wood,
To seek where she might ly dry;
If the mare should chance to fale,
Then the crownes would for her sale.

XXII.

I HAD a little dog, and his name was Blue Bell,
I gave him some work, and he did it very well;
I sent him up stairs to pick up a pin,
He stepped in the coal-scuttle up to the chin.
I sent him to the garden to pick some sage,
He tumbled down and fell in a rage;
I sent him to the cellar, to draw a pot of beer,
He came up again, and said there was none there.

XXIII.

THERE was a little man,
And he woo'd a little maid,
And he said, little maid, will you wed, wed, wed?
I have little more to say,
Than will you, yea or nay,
For least said is soonest mended—ded, ded, ded.

The little maid replied,
Some say a little sighed,
But what shall we have for to eat, eat, eat?
Will the love that you're so rich in,
Make a fire in the kitchen?
Or the little god of Love turn the spit—spit, spit?

XXIV.

I had a little moppet,
I put it in my pocket,
And fed it with corn and hay;
Then came a proud beggar,
And swore he would have her,
And stole my little moppet away.

XXV.

There were two birds sat on a stone,
Fa, la, la, la, lal, de;
One flew-away, and then there was one,
Fa, la, la, la, lal, de;
The other flew after, and then there was none,
Fa, la, la, la, lal de;
And so the poor stone was left all alone,
Fa, la, la, la, lal, de!

XXVI.

There was a little Guinea-pig,
Who, being little, was not big,
He always walked upon his feet,
And never fasted when he eat.

When from a place he ran away,
He never at that place did stay;
And while he ran, as I am told,
He ne'er stood still for young or old.

He often squeak'd, and sometimes vi'lent,
And when he squeak'd he ne'er was silent:
Tho' ne'er instructed by a cat,
He knew a mouse was not a rat.

One day, as I am certified,
He took a whim and fairly died;
And as I'm told by men of sense,
He never has been living since.

XXVII.

Did you not hear of Betty Pringle's pig?
It was not very little, nor yet very big;
The pig sat down upon a dunghill,
And then poor piggy he made his will.

Betty Pringle came to see this pretty pig,
That was not very little, nor yet very big;
This little piggy it lay down and died,
And Betty Pringle sat down and cried.

Then Johnny Pringle buried this very pretty pig,
That was not very little, nor yet very big;
So here's an end of the song of all three,
Johnny Pringle, Betty Pringle, and the little Piggie.

XXVIII.

THREE wise men of Gotham,
Went to sea in a bowl:
And if the bowl had been stronger,
My song would have been longer.

XXIX.

[THE following was most probably taken from a poetical tale in the "Choyce Poems," 12mo. Lond. 1662. As it is a very popular nursery song, I shall give the tale to which I allude in No. 30.]

THREE children sliding on the ice,
Upon a summer's day,
As it fell out, they all fell in,
The rest they ran away.

Now had these children been at home,
Or sliding on dry ground,
Ten thousand pounds to one penny,
They had not all been drown'd.

XXX.

[From "Ovid de Arte Amandi &c. Englished, together with Choice Poems, and rare Pieces of Drollery." 1662.]

SOME Christian people *all* give ear,
Unto the grief of us,
Caused by the death of three children dear;
The which it hapned thus.

And eke there befel an accident,
  By fault of a carpenter's son,
Who to *saw* chips his sharp axe lent,
  Wo woeth the time may Lon—

May London say, wo woeth the carpenter,
  And all such *block-head* fools,
Would he were hang'd up like a serpent here,
  For jesting with edge-tools.

For into the chips there fell a spark,
  Which *put out* in such flames,
That it was known in Southwark,
  Which lies beyond the Thames.

For *lo*, the bridge was wondrous *high*,
  With water underneath,
O'er which as many *fishes* fly,
  As *birds* therein doth breath.

And yet the fire consum'd the bridge,
  Not far from place of landing;
And though the building was full big,
  It *fell down* not-with-*standing*.

And eke into the water fell
  So many pewter dishes,
That a man might have taken up very well
  Both *boil'd* and *roasted* fishes.

And that the *bridge* of London town,
  For building that was sumptuous,
Was *all* by fire *half* burnt down,
  For being too contumptious:

And thus you have all but half my song,
  Pray list to what comes after;
For now I have *cool'd* you with the *fire*,
  I'll *warm* you with the *water*.

I'll tell you what the river's name is,
  Where these children did slide-a,
It was fair London's swiftest Thames,
  That keeps both time and tide-a.

All on the tenth of January,
  To the wonder of much people,
'Twas frozen o'er, that well 'twould bear
  Almost a country steeple.

Three children sliding thereabouts,
  Upon a place *too thin*,
That so at last it did fall *out*,
  That they did all fall *in*.

A great lord there was that laid with the king,
  And with the king great wager makes:
But when he saw he could not win,
  He seight, and would have drawn stakes.

He said it would bear a man for to slide,
  And laid a hundred pound;
The king said it would break, and so it did,
  For three children there were drown'd.

Of which one's head was from his *should-*
  ers stricken, whose name was John,
Who then cry'd out as loud as he could,
  " O Lon-a, Lon-a, London!

" Oh! tut,-tut,-turn from thy sinful race,"
  Thus did his speech decay:
I wonder that in such a case
  He had no more to say.

And thus being drown'd, alack, alack,
  The water ran down their throats,
And stopt their breath three hours by the clock,
  Before they could get any boats.

Ye parents all that *children have,*
  And ye that have none yet;
Preserve your children from the grave,
  And teach them at home to sit.

For had they at a sermon been,
  Or else upon dry ground,
Why then I would have never been seen,
  If that they had been *drown'd.*

Even as a huntsman ties his dogs,
  For fear they should go from him;
So tie your children with severity's clogs,
  Untie 'em, and you'll undo 'em.

God bless our noble parliament,
  And rid them from all fears!
God bless all th' *commons* of this land,
  And God bless *some* o' th' peers!

XXXI.

THERE was an old man in a velvet coat,
He kiss'd a maid and gave her a groat;
The groat was crack'd, and would not go,—
Ah, old man, d'ye serve me so?

XXXII.

THERE was an old man,
And he had a calf,
  And that's half:
He took him out of the stall,
And put him on the wall;
  And that's all.

XXXIII.

I'll tell you a story,
About Jack a Nory;
And now my story's begun:
I'll tell you another
About Jack his brother,
And now my story's done.

XXXIV.

The man in the moon,
Came tumbling down,
And ask'd his way to Norwich.
He went by the south,
And burnt his mouth,
With supping hot pease porridge.

XXXV.

The man in the moon drinks claret,
But he is a dull Jack-a-Dandy;
Would he know a sheep's head from a carrot,
He should learn to drink cider and brandy.

XXXVI.

TOM, Tom, the piper's son,
Stole a pig, and away he run!
The pig was eat, and Tom was beat,
And Tom went roaring down the street!

XXXVII.

THERE was an old woman
Liv'd under a hill,
She put a mouse in a bag,
And sent it to mill;

The miller did swear,
By the point of his knife,
He never took toll
Of a mouse in his life!

XXXVIII.

FOUR and twenty tailors went to kill a snail,
The best man among them durst not touch her tail;
She put out her horns like a little kyloe cow,
Run, tailors run, or she'll kill you all e'en now.

XXXIX.

JACK Sprat could eat no fat,
His wife could eat no lean;
And so, betwixt them both,
They lick'd the platter clean.

XL.

LITTLE Jack Jingle,
He used to live single:
But when he got tired of this kind of life,
He left off being single, and liv'd with his wife.

XLI.

[THE last verse of the following song is popular in our nurseries, and must be of great antiquity, as it is alluded to in MS. Lansd. 760, in a poem of the time of Henry VII.]

COME all ye brisk young bachelors,
That wish to have good wives;
I'd have you be precautious,
How you spend your lives.
For women they are as various,
As the fish are in the sea;
They're ten times more precarious,
Than a winter or summer's day!

When first you begin to court them,
  They're as mild as any dove,
And you will think them,
  Full worthy of your love;
But when you do get married,
  The case is altered then;
For you will find, my friend,
  They can let loose their tongues!

Now Aristotle chose
  A most commodious wife,
As ever was in this land, Sir,
  A partner for his life;
But soon he found out
  'Twas all a hum,
You must not stay to pick them,
  But take them as they come!

Blank or prize 'tis all a chance,
Shut your eyes and then advance!
Whiche'er you touch be pleased at once,
For you must pay, let who will dance.

There was a victim in a cart,
  One day for to be hung;
And his reprieve was granted,
  And the cart was made to stand:
"Come marry a wife and save your life!"
  The judge aloud did cry.

"Oh why should I corrupt my life?"
The victim did reply:
"For here's a crowd of every sort,
And why should I prevent the sport?
The bargain's bad in every part—
The wife's the worst; drive on the cart!"

XLII.

The lion and the unicorn,
Were fighting for the crown;
The lion beat the unicorn,
All round about the town.
Some gave him white bread,
Some gave him plum cake,
And sent him out of town.

XLIII.

Doctor Faustus was a good man,
He whipt his children now and then;
When he whipp'd them he made them dance,
Out of Scotland into France,
Out of France into Spain,
And then he whipp'd them back again!

XLIV.

LITTLE Miss Mopsey,
Sat in the shopsey,
Eating curds and whey;
There came a little spider,
Who sat down beside her,
And frightened little Miss Mopsey away!

XLV.

TOM married a wife on Sunday,
Beat her well on Monday,
Bad was she on Tuesday,
Midling was she on Wednesday,
Worse was she on Thursday,
Dead was she on Friday;
Glad was Tom on Saturday night,
To bury his wife on Sunday.

XLVI.

SOLOMON Grundy,
Born on Monday,
Christened on Tuesday,
Married on Wednesday,
Took ill on Thursday,
Worse on Friday,

Died on Saturday,
Buried on Sunday;
This is the end
Of Solomon Grundy!

XLVII.

There was a crooked man, and he went a crooked mile,
He found a crooked sixpence against a crooked stile;
He bought a crooked cat, which caught a crooked-mouse,
And they all liv'd together in a little crooked house.

XLVIII.

Little blue Betty lived in a den,
She sold good ale to gentlemen:
Gentlemen came every day,
And little blue Betty hopp'd away.
She hopp'd up stairs to make her bed,
And she tumbled down and broke her head.

XLIX.

The fox and his wife they had a great strife,
They never eat mustard in all their whole life;
They eat their meat without fork or knife,
And lov'd to be picking a bone, e-oh!

The fox jumped up on a moonlight night;
The stars they were shining, and all things bright;
Oho! said the fox, it's a very fine night,
For me to go through the town, e-oh!

The fox, when he came to yonder stile,
He lifted his lugs and he listened a while!
Oh, ho! said the fox, it's but a short mile
From this unto yonder wee town, e-oh!

The fox when he came to the farmer's gate,
Who should he see but the farmer's drake;
I love you well for your master's sake,
And long to be picking your bone, e-oh!

The grey goose she ran round the hay-stack,
Oh, ho! said the fox, you are very fat;
You'll grease my beard and ride on my back,
From this into yonder wee town, e-oh!

The farmer's wife she jump'd out of bed,
And out of the window she popped her head!
Oh, husband! oh, husband! the geese are all dead,
For the fox has been through the town, e-oh!

The farmer he loaded his pistol with lead,
And shot the old rogue of a fox through the head;
Ah, ha! said the farmer, I think you're quite dead;
And no more you'll trouble the town, e-oh!

L.

THERE was an old man, who lived in a wood,
As you may plainly see;
He said he could do as much work in a day,
As his wife could do in three.
With all my heart, the old woman said,
If that you will allow,
To-morrow you'll stay at home in my stead,
And I'll go drive the plough.

But you must milk the Tidy cow,
For fear that she go dry;
And you must feed the little pigs,
That are within the sty;
And you must mind the speckled hen,
For fear she lay away;
And you must reel the spool of yarn,
That I spun yesterday.

The old woman took a staff in her hand,
And went to drive the plough;
The old man took a pail in his hand,
And went to milk the cow:
But Tidy hinched, and Tidy flinched,
And Tidy broke his nose,
And Tidy gave him such a blow,
That the blood ran down to his toes!

High! Tidy! Ho! Tidy! high!
    Tidy! stand still,
If ever I milk you Tidy, again,
    'Twill be sore against my will!
He went to feed the little pigs,
    That were within the sty;
He hit his head against the beam,
    And he made the blood to fly.

He went to mind the speckled hen,
    For fear she'd lay astray;
And he forgot the spool of yarn,
    His wife spun yesterday.
So he swore by the sun, the moon, and the stars,
    And the green leaves on the tree;
If his wife didn't do a day's work in her life,
    She should ne'er be rul'd by he.

LI.

THERE was a man in our toone, in our toone, in our toone,
There was a man in our toone, and his name was Billy Pod;
And he played upon an old razor, an old razor, an old razor,
And he played upon an old razor, with my fiddle fiddle fe fum fo.

And his hat it was made of the good roast beef, the
good roast beef, &c.
And his hat it was made of the good roast beef, and his
name was Billy Pod;
And he played upon an old razor, &c. &c.

And his coat it was made of the good fat tripe, the
good fat tripe, the good fat tripe,
And his coat it was made of the good fat tripe, and his
name was Billy Pod;
And he played upon an old razor, &c.

And his breeks they were made of the bawbie baps,
the bawbie baps, &c.
And his breeks they were made of the bawbie baps,
and his name was Billy Pod;
And he played upon an old razor, &c.

And there was a man in tither toone, in tither toone,
in tither toone,
And there was a man in tither toone, and his name
was Edrin Drum;
And he played upon an old laadle, an old laadle, an old
laadle,
And he played upon an old laadle, with my fiddle,
fiddle fe fum fo.

And he eat up all the good roast beef, the good roast
beef, &c. &c.

And he eat up all the good fat tripe, the good fat tripe, &c. &c.

And he eat up all the bawbie baps, &c. and his name was Edrin Drum.

LII.

THERE was a little man,
And he had a little gun,
And his bullets were made of lead, lead, lead.
He went to a brook,
And fired at a duck,
And shot him through the head, head, head.

He carried it home,
To his old wife Joan,
And bid her a fire for to make, make, make.
To roast the little duck,
He'd shot in the brook,
And he'd go and fetch her the drake, drake, drake.

The drake was a swimming,
With his curly tail;
The little man made it his mark, mark, mark!
He let off his gun,
But he fir'd too soon,
And the drake flew away with a quack, quack, quack.

LIII.

Lucy Locket lost her pocket,
Kitty Fisher found it:
Nothing in it, nothing in it,
But the binding round it.

LIV.

Says Aaron to Moses,
Let's cut off our noses:
Says Moses to Aaron,
'Tis the fashion to wear 'em.

LV.

Says Moses to Aaron,
That fellow's a swearing:
Says Aaron to Moses,
He's drunk I supposes.

LVI.

Bessy Bell and Mary Gray,
They were two bonnie lasses:
They built their house upon the lea,
And covered it with rushes.

Bessy kept the garden gate,
  And Mary kept the pantry:
Bessy always had to wait,
  While Mary lived in plenty.

LVII.

My lady Wind, my lady Wind,
Went round about the house to find
  A chink to get her foot in:
She tried the key-hole in the door,
She tried the crevice in the floor,
  And drove the chimney soot in.

And then one night, when it was dark,
She blew up such a tiny spark,
  That all the house was pothered:
From it she rais'd up such a flame,
As flamed away to Belting Lane,
  And White Cross folks were smothered.

And thus when once, my little dears,
A whisper reaches itching ears,
  The same will come, you'll find:
Take my advice, restrain the tongue,
Remember what old nurse has sung
  Of busy lady Wind!

LVIII.

Robin the Bobbin, the big-bellied Ben,
He eat more meat than fourscore men;
He eat a cow, he eat a calf,
He eat a butcher and a half;
He eat a church, he eat a steeple,
He eat the priest and all the people!

LIX.

Peg, Peg, with a wooden leg,
Her father was a miller:
He tossed the dumpling at her head,
And said he could not kill her.

LX.

[The tale of Jack Horner has long been appropriated to the nursery. The four lines which follow are the traditional ones, and they form part of "The pleasant History of Jack Horner, containing his witty Tricks and pleasant Pranks, which he plaied from his Youth to his riper Years," 12mo. a copy of which is in the Bodleian Library.]

Little Jack Horner, sat in the corner,
Eating of Christmas pie:
He put in his thumb, and took out a plum,
And said, "What a brave boy am I!"

LXI.

[THIS nursery song may probably commemorate a part of Tom Thumb's history, extant in a little Danish work, treating of "Swain Tomling, a man no bigger than a thumb, who would be married to a woman three ells and three quarters long." See Mr. Thoms' Preface to "Tom à Lincoln," p. xi.]

I HAD a little husband,
No bigger than my thumb;
I put him in a pint pot,
And then I bade him drum:
I bridled him, and saddled him,
And sent him out of town:
I gave him a pair of garters
To tie up his little hose;
And a little silk handkerchief,
To wipe his little nose.

LXII.

THERE was an old woman who lived in a shoe,
She had so many children she didn't know what to do;
She gave them some broth without any bread,
She whipped them all well and put them to bed.

LXIII.

[The following is a Scotch version of the same song.]

THERE was a wee bit wifie,
Who lived in a shoe;
She had so many bairns,
She kenn'd na what to do.
She gaed to the market
To buy a sheep-head;
When she came back
They were a' lying dead.
She went to the wright
To get them a coffin;
When she came back
They were a' lying laughing.
She gaed up the stair,
To ring the bell;
The bell-rope broke,
And down she fell.

LXIV.

TAFFY was a Welchman, Taffy was a thief;
Taffy came to my house, and stole a piece of beef:
I went to Taffy's house, Taffy was not at home;
Taffy came to my house, and stole a marrow-bone.

I went to Taffy's house, Taffy was not in;
Taffy came to my house, and stole a silver pin:
I went to Taffy's house, Taffy was in bed,
I took up a poker and flung it at his head.

LXV.

OLD Dr. Foster went to Gloster,
To preach the word of God:
When he came there, he sat in his chair,
And gave all the people a nod.

LXVI.

MARY had a pretty bird,
Feathers bright and yellow,
Slender legs,—upon my word
He was a pretty fellow.

The sweetest note he always sung,
Which much delighted Mary;
She often where the cage was hung,
Sate to hear her canary.

LXVII.

THE carrion crow, he sat upon an oak,
And he called the tailor a cheating folk ;
" Sing heigho, the carrion crow,
Fol de rol, de rol, de rol, de rhino."

Wife, fetch me my good strong bow,
That I may kill the carrion crow.
" Sing heigho," &c.

The tailor shot, and missed his mark,
And shot the old sow through the heart.
" Sing heigho," &c.

LXVIII.

[Another version of one given p. 23.]

THERE was an old woman sat spinning,
And that 's the first beginning ;
She had a calf,
And that 's half ;
She took it by the tail,
And threw it over the wall,
And that 's all !

LXIX.

Some little mice sat in a barn to spin;
Pussy came by, and she popped her head in:
"Shall I come in, and cut your threads off?"
"Oh! no, kind sir, you will snap our heads off!"

LXX.

Three blind mice, the three blind mice,
They all ran after the farmer's wife,
Who cut off their tails with the carving-knife.

LXXI.

St. Dunstan, as the story goes,
Once pulled the devil by the nose,
With red-hot tongs, which made him roar,
That he was heard ten miles or more.

LXXII.

As I was walking o'er little Moorfields,
I saw St. Paul's a running on wheels,
With a fee, fo, fum.
Then for further frolics I'll go to France,
While Jack shall sing and his wife shall dance,
With a fee, fo, fum.

LXXIII.

TOMMY TROT, a man of law,
Sold his bed and lay upon straw:
Sold the straw and slept on grass,
To buy his wife a looking-glass.

LXXIV.

THERE was a lady lov'd a swine,
  Honey, quoth she,
Pig, Hog, wilt thou be mine?
  Hoogh, quoth he.

I'll build thee a silver sty,
  Honey, quoth she;
And in it thou shalt lie,
  Hoogh, quoth he.

Pinn'd with a silver pin,
  Honey, quoth she;
That you may go out and in,
  Hoogh, quoth he.

Wilt thou have me now,
  Honey? quoth she;
Hoogh, hoogh, hoogh, quoth he,
  And went his way.

LXXV.

THERE was an old woman, as I've heard tell,
She went to market her eggs for to sell;
She went to market all on a market day.
And she fell asleep on the king's highway.

There came by a pedlar whose name was Stout,
He cut her petticoats all round about;
He cut her petticoats up to the knees,
Which made the old woman to shiver and freeze.

When this little woman first did wake,
She began to shiver and she began to shake,
She began to wonder and she began to cry,
"Lauk a mercy on me, this is none of I!

"But if it be I, as I do hope it be,
I've a little dog at home, and he'll know me;
If it be I, he'll wag his little tail,
And if it be not I, he'll loudly bark and wail!"

Home went the little woman all in the dark,
Up got the little dog, and he began to bark;
He began to bark, so she began to cry,
"Lauk a mercy on me, this can't be I!"

LXXVI.

Little Mary Ester sat upon a tester,
Eating curds and whey;
There came a spider, and sat down beside her,
And frightened little Mary Ester away!

LXXVII.

[This nursery rhyme is quoted in Beaumont and Fletcher's *Bonduca*, Act. v. sc. 2.]

Sing a song of sixpence,
A pocket full of rye;
Four-and-twenty blackbirds
Baked in a pie;

When the pie was opened,
The birds began to sing;
Was not that a dainty dish
To set before the king?

The king was in the parlour
Counting out his money;
The queen was in her closet
Eating bread and honey;

The maid was in the garden
Hanging out the clothes,
Up comes a little blackbird,
And snaps off her nose.

LXXVIII.

A CARRION crow sat on an oak,
Watching a tailor shape his cloak.
"Wife," cried he, "bring me my bow,
That I may shoot you carrion crow."

The tailor shot and miss'd his mark,
And shot his own sow through the heart.
"Wife, bring me some brandy in a spoon,
For our old sow is in a swoon."*

LXXIX.

[THIS apparently alludes to the celebrated General Monk; but as it seems to be altogether apocryphal, I have not admitted it into the historical class.]

LITTLE General Monk
Sat upon a trunk,
Eating a crust of bread;
There fell a hot coal
And burnt in his clothes a hole,
Now Little General Monk is dead.
Keep always from the fire:
If it catch your attire,
You too, like Monk, will be dead.

* See p. 42.

LXXX.

Little Jenny Wren fell sick upon a time,
When in came Robin Red-breast, and brought her
bread and wine;
"Eat, Jenny, drink, Jenny, all shall be thine!"
Then Jenny she got better, and stood upon her feet,
And says to little Robin, "I love thee not a bit!"
Then Robin he was angry and flew upon a twig,
"Hoot upon thee, fie upon thee, ungrateful chit!"

LXXXI.

THE STORY OF CATSKIN.

[As related by an old nurse, aged eighty-one. The story is of oriental origin; but the song, as recited, was so very imperfect, that a few necessary additions and alterations have been made.]

There once was a gentleman grand,
Who lived at his country-seat;
He wanted an heir to his land,
For he'd nothing but daughters yet.

His lady's again in the way,
So she said to her husband with joy;
"I hope some or other fine day,
To present you, my dear, with a boy."

The gentleman answered gruff,
  "If 't should turn out a maid or a mouse,
For of both we have more than enough,
  She shan't stay to live in my house."

The lady at this declaration,
  Almost fainted away with pain;
But what was her sad consternation,
  When a sweet little girl came again!

She sent her away to be nurs'd,
  Without seeing her gruff papa;
And when she was old enough,
  To a school she was packed away.

Fifteen summers are fled,
  Now she left good Mrs. Jervis;
To see home she was forbid,—
  She determined to go and seek service

Her dresses so grand and so gay,
  She carefully rolled in a knob;
Which she hid in a forest away,
  And put on a Catskin robe.

She knock'd at a castle gate,
  And pray'd for charity;
They sent her some meat on a plate,
  And kept her a scullion to be.

My lady look'd long in her face,
   And prais'd her great beauty;
I'm sorry I've no better place,
   And you must our scullion be.

So Catskin was under the cook,
   A very sad life she led,
For often a ladle she took,
   And broke poor Catskin's head.

There is now a grand ball to be,
   When ladies their beauties show;
"Mrs. Cook," said Catskin, "dear me!
   How much I should like to go."

"You go with your Catskin-robe,
   You dirty impudent slut!
Among the fine ladies and lords,
   A very fine figure you'd cut!"

A basin of water she took,
   And dashed in poor Catskin's face;
But briskly her ears she shook,
   And went to her hiding place.

She washed every stain from her skin,
   In some cristal waterfall;
Then put on a beautiful dress,
   And hasted away to the ball.

When she entered, the ladies were mute,
  Overcome by her figure and face;
But the lord, her young master, at once
  Fell in love with her beauty and grace!

He pray'd her his partner to be,
  She said, "Yes," with a sweet smiling glance;
All night with no other lady
  But Catskin, our young lord would dance.

"Pray tell me, fair maid, where you live,"
  For now was the sad parting time;
But she no other answer would give,
  Than this distych of mystical rhyme,—

"Kind sir, if the truth I must tell,
At the sign of the basin of water I dwell."

Then she flew from the ball-room, and put
  On her Catskin robe again;
And slipt in unseen by the cook,
  Who little thought where she had been.

The young lord the very next day,
  To his mother his passion betray'd,
And declared he never would rest,
  Till he'd found out his beautiful maid!

There's another grand ball to be,
  Where ladies their beauty show;

"Mrs. Cook," said Catskin, "dear me,
How much I should like to go."

"You go with your Catskin robe,
You dirty, impudent slut!
Among the fine ladies and lords,
A very fine figure you'd cut!"

In a rage the ladle she took,
And broke poor Catskin's head;
But off she went shaking her ears,
And swift to her forest she fled.

She washed every blood stain off,
In some cristal waterfall;
Put on a more beautiful dress,
And hasted away to the ball.

My lord at the ball-room door,
Was waiting with pleasure and pain;
He longed to see nothing so much,
As the beautiful Catskin again.

When he asked her to dance, she again
Said "Yes," with her first smiling glance;
And again all the night my young lord,
With none but fair Catskin did dance!

"Pray tell me," said he, "where you live;"
For now 'twas the parting time;

But she no other answer would give,
  Than this distych of mystical rhyme,—

"Kind sir, if the truth I must tell,
At the sign of the broken ladle I dwell."

Then she flew from the ball, and put on
  Her Catskin robe again;
And slipt in unseen by the cook,
  Who little thought where she had been.

My lord did again the next day,
  Declare to his mother his mind,
That he never more happy should be,
  Unless he his charmer should find.

Now another grand ball is to be,
  When ladies their beauty show:
"Mrs. Cook," said Catskin, "dear me,
  How much I should like to go."

"You go with your Catskin robe,
  You impudent, dirty slut!
Among the fine ladies and lords,
  A very fine figure you'd cut!"

In a fury she took the skimmer,
  And broke poor Catskin's head!
But heart-whole and lively as ever,
  Away to her forest she fled!

She washed the stains of blood,
  In some cristal waterfall;
Then put on her most beautiful dress,
  And hasted away to the ball.

My lord at the ball-room door,
  Was waiting with pleasure and pain;
He longed to see nothing so much,
  As the beautiful Catskin again.

When he asked her to dance, she again
  Said "Yes," with her first smiling glance;
And all the night long, my young lord
  With none but fair Catskin would dance!

"Pray tell me, fair maid, where you live;"
  For now was the parting time:
But she no other answer would give,
  Than this distych of mystical rhyme,—

"Kind sir, if the truth I must tell,
At the sign of the broken strimmer I dwell."

Then she flew from the ball, and threw on
  Her catskin-cloak again;
And slipt in unseen by the cook,
  Who little thought where she had been.

But not by my lord unseen,
  For this time he follow'd too fast;

And hid in the forest green,
  Saw the strange things that past!

Next day he took to his bed,
  And sent for the doctor to come;
And begg'd him no other than Catskin,
  Might come into his room!

He told him how dearly he lov'd her,
  Not to have her his heart would break;
Then the doctor kindly promis'd,
  To the proud old lady to speak.

There's a struggle of pride and love,
  For she fear'd her son would die;
But pride at the last did yield,
  And love had the mastery!

Then my lord got quickly well,
  When he was his charmer to vow;
And Catskin before a twelvemonth,
  Of a young lord was brought to bed.

To a way-faring woman and child,
  Lady Catskin one day sent an alms;
The nurse did the errand, and carried
  The sweet little lord in her arms.

The child gave the alms to the child,
  This was seen by the old lady mother;

"Only see," said that wicked old woman,
 "How the beggars' brats take to each other!"

This throw went to Catskin's heart,
 She flung herself down on her knees,
And pray'd her young master and lord,
 To seek out her parents would please.

They set out in my lord's own coach,
 And travell'd; but nought befell,
Till they reach'd the town hard by,
 Where Catskin's father did dwell.

They put up at the head inn,
 Where Catskin was left alone;
But my lord went to try if her father,
 His natural child would own.

When folks are away, in short time
 What great alterations appear!
For the cold touch of death had all chill'd,
 The hearts of her sisters dear.

Her father repented too late,
 And the loss of his youngest bemoan'd;
In his old and childless state,
 He his pride and cruelty own'd!

The old gentleman sat by the fire,
 And hardly looked up at my lord;

He had no hopes of comfort,
  A stranger could afford.

But my lord drew a chair close by,
  And said, in a feeling tone,
"Have you not, sir, a daughter I pray,
  You never would see or own?"

The old man alarm'd, cried aloud,
  "A hardened sinner am I!
I would give all my worldly goods,
  To see her before I die!"

Then my lord brought his wife and child,
  To their home and parents' face;
Who fell down and thanks return'd
  To God, for his mercy and grace!

The bells ringing up in the tower,
  Are sending a sound to the heart;
There's a charm in the old church bells,
  Which nothing in life can impart!

LXXXII.

Says Robin to Jenny, "if you will be mine,
We'll have cherry tart, and drink currant wine."
So Jenny consented,—the day was nam'd,
The joyful news the cock proclaim'd:

Together came the Rook and Lark,
One was parson, the other clerk:
The goldfinch gave the bride away,
Who promised always to obey:
The feathered tenants of the air,
Towards the feast gave each a share;
Some brought grain, and some brought meat,
Some brought savours, some brought sweet:
And as it was most pleasant weather,
The jovial party dined together;
And long did Robin and his mate,
Live in the happy married state.
Till, doleful to relate! one day
A hawk with Jenny flew away,
And Robin, by the cruel sparrow,
Was shot quite dead with bow and arrow.

LXXIII.

[The tale of Simple Simon forms one of the chap-books, but the following verses are those generally sung in the nursery.]

SIMPLE Simon met a pieman,
  Going to the fair:
Says Simple Simon to the pieman,
  "Let me taste your ware."

Says the pieman to Simple Simon,
  "Shew me first your penny."
Says Simple Simon to the pieman,
  "I have not got any."

Simple Simon went to town,
  To buy a piece of meat:
He tied it to his horse's tail,
  To keep it clean and sweet.

Simple Simon went out fishing,
  For to catch a whale:
All the water he had got
  Was in his mother's pail.

Simple Simon went to look
  If plums grew on a thistle;
He pricked his fingers very much,
  Which made poor Simon whistle.

LXXIV.

THERE was an old woman of Norwich,
Who lived on nothing but porridge!
    Parading the town,
    She turned cloak into gown!
This thrifty old woman of Norwich.

LXXXV.

THERE was an old woman of Leeds,
Who spent all her time in good deeds;
She worked for the poor,
Till her fingers were sore,
This pious old woman of Leeds!

LXXXVI.

OLD mother Hubbard,
Went to the cupboard,
To get her poor dog a bone;
But when she came there,
The cupboard was bare,
And so the poor dog had none.

She went to the baker's
To buy him some bread,
But when she came back
The poor dog was dead.

She went to the joiner's
To buy him a coffin,
But when she came back
The poor dog was laughing.

She took a clean dish
  To get him some tripe,
But when she came back
  He was smoking his pipe.

She went to the ale-house
  To get him some beer,
But when she came back
  The dog sat in a chair.

She went to the tavern
  For white wine and red,
But when she came back
  The dog stood on his head.

She went to the hatter's
  To buy him a hat,
But when she came back
  He was feeding the cat.

She went to the barber's
  To buy him a wig,
But when she came back
  He was dancing a jig.

She went to the fruiterer's
  To buy him some fruit,
But when she came back
  He was playing the flute.

She went to the tailor's
  To buy him a coat,
But when she came back
  He was riding a goat.

She went to the cobler's
  To buy him some shoes,
But when she came back
  He was reading the news.

She went to the sempstress
  To buy him some linen,
But when she came back
  The dog was spinning.

She went to the hosier's
  To buy him some hose,
But when she came back
  He was dress'd in his clothes.

The dame made a curtsey,
  The dog made a bow;
The dame said, your servant,
  The dog said, bow, wow.

LXXVII.

Old King Cole
Was a merry old soul,
And a merry old soul was he;
And he called for his pipe,
And he called for his glass,
And he called for his fiddlers three.
And every fiddler, he had a fine fiddle,
And a very fine fiddle had he;
" Tweedle dee, tweedle dee," said the fiddlers.
Oh there's none so rare,
As can compare,
With King Cole and his fiddlers three!

LXXIX.

Tom he was a piper's son,
He learn'd to play when he was young,
And all the tunes that he could play,
Was " Over the hills and far away;"
Over the hills, and a great way off,
And the wind will blow my top-knot off.

Now Tom with his pipe made such a noise,
That he pleas'd both the girls and boys,
And they stopp'd to hear him play,
" Over the hills and far away."

Tom with his pipe did play with such skill,
That those who heard him could never keep still;
Whenever they heard they began for to dance,
Even pigs on their hind legs would after him prance.

As Dolly was milking her cow one day,
Tom took out his pipe and began for to play;
So Doll and the cow danced the Cheshire round,
Till the pail was broke and the milk ran on the ground.

He met old dame Trot with a basket of eggs,
He used his pipe and she used her legs;
She danced about till the eggs were all broke,
She began for to fret, but he laughed at the joke.

He saw a cross fellow was beating an ass,
Heavy laden with pots, pans, dishes, and glass;
He took out his pipe and played them a tune.
And the jackass's load was lightened full soon.

LXXXIX.

There was a lady all skin and bone,
Sure such a lady was never known:
This lady went to church one day,
She went to church all for to pray.

And when she came to the church stile,
She sat to rest a little while:
When she came to the church-yard,
There the bells so loud she heard.

When she came to the church door,
She stopt to rest a little more;
When she came the church within,
The parson pray'd 'gainst pride and sin.

On looking up, on looking down,
She saw a dead man on the ground:
And from his nose unto his chin,
The worms crawl'd out, the worms crawl'd in.*

Then she unto the parson said,
Shall I be so when I am dead?
Oh yes! oh yes! the parson said,
You will be so when you are dead.

XC.

Little John Jiggy Jag,
He rode a penny nag,
And went to Wigan to woo:

---

* This line has been adopted in the modern ballad of "Alonzo and the fair Imogene." The version given above was obtained from Lincolnshire, and differs slightly from the one in "Gammer Gurton's Garland," 8vo. Lond. 1810, p. 29-30.

When he came to a beck,
He fell and broke his neck,—
  Johnny, how dost thou now?

I made him a hat,
Of my coat-lap,
  And stockings of pearly blue:
A hat and a feather,
To keep out cold weather;
  So, Johnny, how dost thou now?

XCI.

SATURDAY-night my wife did die,
  I buried her on the Sunday,
I courted another a coming from church,
  And married her on the Monday.
On Tuesday night I stole a horse,
  On Wednesday was apprehended,
On Thursday I was tried and cast,
  And on Friday I was hanged.

XCII.

LITTLE Tom Trigger,
Before he was bigger,
  Thought he would go out with his gun;

Left off bow and arrows,
With which he shot sparrows,
And said he would have some fun.

He shot at a pig,
That was not very big,
But pig away did run;
Says he, to be sure,
I am not very poor,
I'll put some more shot in my gun.

He shot at a cat,
That had caught a rat,
And hit her right on the pate;
I'll have your furry skin
To put my powder in,
Your venison, no matter for that.

He started a hare,
The people did stare,
Says he, I'll have you for my dinner;
It being almost dark,
He missed his mark,
For he was a young beginner.

He came to a stile,
A man all the while
A pitchfork had in his hand;
Says he, give me the gun,
But he began to run,
All over the ploughed land.

Unhappy was his lot,
Into a hedge he got,
The man came behind to beat him;
Tom cannot get through,
He had the man in view,
But he contrived to cheat him.

A house was in the vale,
And Margery sold ale,
Says he, I'll have some beer;
Soon it will be night,
And not a bit of light,
My roundabout way home to cheer.

A sow in the sty,
As Tommy came by,
Was calling her pigs to repose;
Says Tom, I love fun,
And at the pigs did run,
But fell down and hurt his nose.

Margery came out,
To see what it was about,
And she said, Master Tommy, O fye!
He took up his gun,
And he began to run,
From the pigs that were in the sty.

Tom at last got home,
He would no longer roam,
And his mother began to scold;

Now he plays at taw,
Sometimes at see-saw,
  And is not quite so bold.

Tom and his dog Tray,
In the month of May,
  Went to play with a ball,
Which he threw up to the sky,
Yet not so very high,
  It soon came down with a fall.

He had a little stick,
It was not very thick,
  He hit the ball to make it go faster;
His little dog Tray,
Soon scampered away,
  To bring the ball back to his master.

He got up a tree,
As high as may be,
  Some eggs from a nest to obtain;
A bough bent in two,
(You see it in the view),
  And he fell to the ground in great pain.

A doctor they did call
To cure him of the fall,
  A long while he kept his bed;
At last he got well
Of all that him befel,
  So this time he shall not be dead.

Tom has now got better,
Writes a pretty letter,
  And is always reading his book;
He is not quite so wild,
As when he was a child
  And no pains with his learning he took.

XCIII.

There was a frog liv'd in a well,
  Kitty alone, Kitty alone,
There was a frog liv'd in a well,
  Kitty alone, and I.
There was a frog liv'd in a well,
And a farce* mouse in a mill,
  Cock me cary, Kitty alone,
  Kitty alone and I.

This frog he would a wooing ride,
  Kitty alone, &c.
This frog he would a wooing ride,
And on a snail he got astride.
  Cock me cary, &c.

---

* Merry.

He rode till he came to my Lady Mouse hall,
  Kitty alone, &c.
He rode till he came to my Lady Mouse hall,
And there he did both knock and call,
  Cock me cary, &c.

Quoth he, Miss Mouse, I'm come to thee,
  Kitty alone, &c.
Quoth he, Miss Mouse, I'm come to thee,
To see if thou canst fancy me,
  Cock me cary, &c.

Quoth she, answer I'll give you none,
  Kitty alone, &c.
Quoth she, answer I'll give you none,
Until my uncle Rat come home,
  Cock me cary, &c.

And when her uncle Rat came home,
  Kitty alone, &c.
And when her uncle Rat came home,
Who's been here since I've been gone?
  Cock me cary, &c.

Sir, there's been a worthy gentleman,
  Kitty alone, &c.
Sir, there's been a worthy gentleman,
That's been here since you've been gone,
  Cock me cary, &c.

The frog he came whistling through the brook,
  Kitty alone, &c.
The frog he came whistling through the brook,
And there he met with a dainty duck.
  Cock me cary, &c.

This duck she swallow'd him up with a pluck,
  Kitty alone, Kitty alone,
This duck she swallow'd him up with a pluck,
So there's an end of my history book.
  Cock me cary, Kitty alone,
  Kitty alone and I.

XCIV.

THERE was an old woman toss'd up in a blanket,
  Ninety-nine times as high as the moon:
But where she was going no mortal could tell,
  For under her arm she carried a broom.

Old woman, old woman, old woman, said I,
  Whither, ah! whither, whither so high?
Oh! I'm sweeping the cobwebs off the sky,
  And I'll be with you by and by.

XCV.

THERE was an old woman,
And she sold puddings and pies:
She went to the mill,
And the dust flew in her eyes:
Hot pies and cold pies to sell!
Wherever she goes,
You can follow her by the smell.

XCVI.

OLD Mother Niddity Nod swore by the pudding-bag,
She would go to Stoken Church fair;
And then old Father Peter, said he would meet her,
Before she got half way there.

XCVII.

GILES Collins he said to his old mother,
Mother, come bind up my head;
And send to the parson of our parish,
For to-morrow I shall be dead, dead,
For to-morrow I shall be dead.

His mother she made him some water-gruel,
And stirred it round with a spoon;
Giles Collins he ate up his water-gruel,
And died before 'twas noon,
And died before 'twas noon.

Lady Anna was sitting at her window,
Mending her night-robe and coif;
She saw the very prettiest corpse,
She'd seen in all her life, life,
She'd seen in all her life.

What bear ye there, ye six strong men,
Upon your shoulders so high?
We bear the body of Giles Collins,
Who for love of you did die, die,
Who for love of you did die.

Set him down! set him down! Lady Anna she cry'd,
On the grass that grows so green;
To-morrow before the clock strikes ten,
My body shall lie by his'n, his'n,
My body shall lie by his'n.

Lady Anna was buried in the east
Giles Collins was buried in the west;
There grew a lily from Giles Collins,
That touch'd Lady Anna's breast, breast,
That touch'd Lady Anna's breast.

There blew a cold north-easterly wind,
  And cut this lily in twain;
Which never there was seen before,
  And it never will again, again,
    And it never will again.

XCVIII.

Little Bo-peep has lost her sheep,
  And can't tell where to find them:
Let them alone, and they'll come home,
  And bring their tails behind them.

Little Bo-peep fell fast asleep,
  And dreamt she heard them bleating:
But when she awoke, she found it a joke,
  For they still were all fleeting.

Then up she took her little crook,
  Determin'd for to find them;
She found them indeed, but it made her heart bleed,
  For they'd left all their tails behind 'em.

It happen'd one day, as Bo-peep did stray,
  Unto a meadow hard by:
There she espy'd their tails side by side,
  All hung on a tree to dry.

She heav'd a sigh, and wip'd her eye,
  And over the hillocks went stump-o;
And tried what she could, as a shepherdess should,
  To tack again each to its rump-o.

XCIX.

JOHN COOK had a little grey mare; he, haw, hum!
Her back stood up, and her bones they were bare; he,
    haw, hum.

John Cook was riding up Shuter's bank; he, haw, hum.
And there his nag did kick and prank; he, haw, hum.

John Cook was riding up Shuter's hill; he haw, hum:
His mare fell down, and she made her will; he, haw, hum.

The bridle and saddle were laid on the shelf; he, ha, hum:
If you want any more you may sing it yourself; he,
    haw, hum.

C.

THERE was a mad man and he had a mad wife,
  And they liv'd in a mad town:
And they had children three at a birth,
  And mad they were every one.

The father was mad, the mother was mad,
And the children mad beside;
And they all got on a mad horse,
And madly they did ride.

They rode by night and they rode by day,
Yet never a one of them fell;
They rode so madly all the way,
Till they came to the gates of hell.

Old Nick was glad to see them so mad,
And gladly let them in:
But he soon grew sorry to see them so merry,
And let them out again.

CI.

THERE was an old man, and he liv'd in a wood;
And his lazy son Jack would snooze till noon:
Nor followed his trade, although it was good,
With a bill and stump for making of brooms, green brooms;
With a bill and a stump for making of brooms.

One morn in a passion, and sore with vexation,
He swore he would fire the room,
If he did not get up and go to his work,
And fall to the cutting of brooms, green brooms, &c.

Then Jack arose and slipt on his clothes,
  And away to the woods very soon,
Where he made up his pack, and put it on his back,
  Crying, Maids, do you want any brooms? green
    brooms, &c.

Third Class.—Jingles.

CII.

Hub a dub dub,
Three men in a tub;
The butcher, the baker,
The candlestick-maker,
They all fell out of a rotten potato.

CIII.

Little Jack-a-dandy,
Loved plum cake, and sugar-candy,
He bought some at a grocer's shop,
And out he came, hop hop hop.

CIV.

Ding, dong, bell,
Puss is in the well!
Who put her in,
Little Tommy Lin:

Who pulled her out,
Dog with long snout;
What a trick was that,
To drown my granny's cat,
Who never did any harm,
But catch the mice in the barn.

CV.

DINGTY diddledy,
My mammy's maid,
She stole oranges,
I am afraid;
Some in her pocket,
Some in her sleeve,
She stole oranges,
I do believe.

CVI.

COCK a doodle doo,
My dame has lost her shoe;
And master's lost his fiddling stick,
And don't know what to do.

Cock a doodle doo,
What is my dame to do?
Till master finds his fiddling stick
She'll dance without her shoe.

Cock a doodle doo,
My dame has found her shoe,
And master's found his fiddling stick,
Sing doodle doodle doo.

Cock a doodle doo,
My dame will dance with you,
While master fiddles his fiddling stick,
For dame and doodle doo.

CVII.

Hey ding a ding, what shall I sing?
How many holes in a skimmer?
Four-and-twenty,—my stomach is empty;
Pray, mamma, give me some dinner.

CVIII.

Deedle, deedle, dumpling, my son John,
Went to the bed with his trousers on;
One shoe off, the other shoe on,
Deedle, deedle, dumpling, my son John.

CIX.

FEEDUM, fiddledum fee,
The cat's got into the tree.
Pussy come down,
Or I'll crack your crown,
And toss you into the sea.

CX.

YANKEE Doodle came to town,
Upon a Kentish poney;
He stuck a feather in his hat,
And called him Macaroni.

CXI.

COME dance a jig
To my Granny's pig,
With a raudy, rowdy, dowdy;
Come dance a jig,
To my Granny's pig,
And Pussey cat shall crowdy [i. e. fiddle.]

CXII.

[From Devonshire.]

Driddlety drum, driddlety drum,
There you see the beggars are come;
Some are here and some are there,
And some are gone to Chidlely fair.

CXIII.

[The following may possibly be a game, but I am without any evidence for so attributing it.]

Intery, mintery, cutery-corn,
Apple seed and apple thorn;
Wine, brier, limber-lock,
Five geese in a flock,
Sit and sing by a spring,
O-U-T, and in again.

CXIV.

A cat came fiddling out of a barn,
With a pair of bag-pipes under her arm;
She could sing nothing but fiddle cum fee.
The mouse has married the humble bee;
Pipe cat, dance mouse,
We'll have a wedding at our good house.

CXV.

HEY, dorolot, dorolot!
  Hey dorolay, dorolay!
Hey, my bonny boat, bonny boat,
  Hey, drag away, drag away!

CXVI.

SEEK a thing, give a thing,
The old man's gold ring;
Lie butt, lie ben,
Lie among the dead men.

CXVII.

HIE! diddle diddle,
The cat and the fiddle,
The cow jumped over the moon,
The little dog laughed to see such sport,
While the dish ran after the spoon.

CXVIII.

CRIPPLE Dick upon a stick,
  And Sandy on a sow,
Riding away to Galloway,
  To buy a pound o' woo.

CXIX.

FIDDLE-de-dee, fiddle-de-dee,
The fly shall marry the humble bee.
They went to the church, and married was she,
The fly has married the humble bee.

CXX.

[*Magot-pie* is the original name of the chattering and ominous bird. See *Macbeth*, Act iii. sc. 4, where the same word is used.]

ROUND about, round about,
Maggotty pie,
My father loves good ale,
And so do I.

CXXI.

DOODLEDY, doodledy, doodledy, dan,
I'll have a piper to be my good man;
And if I get less meat, I shall get game,
Doodledy, doodledy, doodledy, dan.

CXXII.

[From Shropshire.]

One, two, three,
I love coffee,
And Billy loves tea.
How good you be,
One, two, three,
I love coffee,
And Billy loves tea.

CXXIII.

Dick and Tom, Will and John,
Brought me from Nottingham.

CXXIV.

One-ery, two-ery,
Ziccary zan;
Hollow bone, crack a bone,
Ninery ten:
Spittery spot,
It must be done;
Twiddleum twaddleum,
Twenty-one.

Hink spink, the puddings stink,
The fat begins to fry,
Nobody at home, but jumping Joan,
Father, mother and I.
Stick, stock, stone dead,
Blind man can't see,
Every knave, will have a slave,
You or I must be he.

CXXV.

Tommy Tibule, Harry Wibule,
Tommy Tissile, Harry Whistle,
Little wee, wee, wee.

CXXVI.

[A Scottish ditty, sung on whirling round a piece of lighted paper to a child.]

Dingle, dingle, doosey;
The cat's in the well;
The dog's away to Bellingen,
To buy the bairn a bell.

CXXVII.

[Water-skimming.]

A DUCK and a drake,
A nice barley cake,
With a penny to pay the old baker:
A hop and a skotch,
Is another notch,
Slitherum, slatherum, take her.

CXXVIII.

GILLY Silly Jarter,
Who has lost a garter?
In a shower of rain,
The miller found it,
The miller ground it,
And the miller gave it to Silly again.

CXXIX.

SEE, saw, Margery Daw,
Jackey shall have a new master;
He shall have only a penny a-day,
Because he can work no faster.

CXXX.

[See Jamieson's *Glossary*, voc. zickety, and Blackwood's *Edinburgh Magazine*, Aug. 1821, p. 36.]

Zickety, dickety, dock,
The mouse ran up the nock;
The nock struck one,
Down the mouse run,
Zickety, dickety, dock.

CXXXI.

See, Saw, Margery Daw,
Sold her bed and lay upon straw;
Was not she a dirty slut,
To sell her bed and lie upon dirt?

CXXXII.

Ding, dong, darrow,
The cat and the sparrow;
The little dog has burnt his tail,
And he shall be hang'd tomorrow.

CXXXIII.

Pussicat, wussicat, with a white foot,
When is your wedding, and I'll come to't.
The beer's to brew, the bread's to bake,
Pussy cat, pussy cat, don't be too late!

CXXXIV.

Ride to the market to buy a fat pig,
  Home again, home again, jiggety-jig;
Ride to the market to buy a fat hog,
  Home again, home again, jiggety-jog.

CXXXV.

Leg over leg,
  As the dog went to Dover;
When he came to a stile,
  Jump he went over.

Fourth Class.—Riddles.

CXXXVI.

[A HEDGEHOG.]

As I went over Lincoln bridge,
I met mister Rusticap;
Pins and needles on his back,
A going to Thorney fair.

CXXXVII.

[A BED.]

FORMED long ago, yet made to day,
 Employed while others sleep;
What few would like to give away,
 Nor any wish to keep.

CXXXVIII.

[A CINDER.]

A RIDDLE, a riddle, as I suppose,
A hundred eyes, and never a nose.

CXXXIX.

[A WELL.]

As round as an apple, as deep as a cup,
And all the king's horses can't pull it up.

CXL.

[AN EGG.]

HUMPTY DUMPTY sate on a wall,
Humpti dumpti had a great fall;
Three score men and three score more,
Cannot place Humpty dumpty as he was before.

CXLI.

Goosy goosy gander!
Where shall I wander?
Up stairs and down stairs,
And in my lady's chamber;
There I met an old man,
That would not say his prayers.
I took him by the left leg,
And threw him down stairs.

CXLII.

[A RAINBOW.]

[The allusion to Oliver Cromwell satisfactorily fixes the date of this riddle to belong to the seventeenth century.]

PURPLE, yellow, red and green,
The king cannot reach it nor the queen;
Nor can old Noll, whose power's so great,
Tell me this riddle while I count eight.

CXLIII.

[A CANDLE.]

LITTLE Nancy Etticoat,
In a white petticoat;
The longer she stands,
The shorter she grows.

CXLIV.

[PAIR OF TONGS.]

Long legs, crooked thighs,
Little head and no eyes.

CXLV.

[ONE LEG IS A LEG OF MUTTON; TWO LEGS, A MAN; THREE LEGS, A STOOL; FOUR LEGS, A DOG.]

Two legs sat upon three legs,
With one leg in his lap;
In comes four legs,
And runs away with one leg.
Up jumps two legs,
Catches up three legs,
Throws it after four legs,
And makes him bring back one leg.

CXLVI.

As I was going to sell my eggs,
I met a man with bandy legs,
Bandy legs and crooked toes,
I tripped up his heels and he fell on his nose.

CXLVII.

Pease-porridge hot, pease-porridge cold,
Pease-porridge in the pot, nine days old.
Spell me *that* in four letters.

CXLVIII.

[TEETH AND GUMS.]

THIRTY white horses on a red hill.
Now they tramp, now they champ, now they stand still,

CXLIX.

[A CHERRY.]

As I went through the garden gap,
Who should I meet but Dick Red-cap!
A stick in his hand, a stone in his throat.
If you'll tell me this riddle, I'll give you a groat.

CL.

ELIZABETH, Elspeth, Betsy and Bess,
They all went together to seek a bird's nest.
They found a bird's nest with five eggs in,
They all took one, and left four in.

CLI.

As I was going to St. Ives,
I met a man with seven wives,
Every wife had seven sacks,
Every sack had seven cats,
Every cat had seven kits:
Kits, cats, sacks, and wives,
How many were there going to St. Ives?

CLII.

SEE, see! what shall I see?
A horse's head where his tail should be.

CLIII.

I HAD a little castle upon the sea-side,
One half was water, the other was land;
I open'd my little castle door, and guess what I found;
I found a fair lady with a cup in her hand.
The cup was gold, filled with wine;
Drink fair lady, and thou shalt be mine.

CLIV.

WHEN I went up sandy-hill,
I met a sandy boy;
I cut his throat, I sucked his blood,
And left his skin a hanging-o.

CLV.

[THE HOLLY TREE.]

HIGHTY, tighty, paradighty clothed in green,
The king could not read it, no more could the queen;
They sent for a wise man out of the East,
Who said it had horns, but was not a beast!

CLVI.

I HAD a little sister, they call'd her peep, peep,
She waded the waters deep, deep, deep,
She climbed up the mountains high, high, high,
Poor little creature she wanted an eye.

Fifth Class.—Proverbs.

CLVII.

A SEMPSTRESS that sews,
And would make her work redde [i.e. scarce],
Must use a long needle,
And a short thread.

CLVIII.

[The following old saw is generally believed to refer to the Teutonic method of numbering. See Brand's *Popular Antiquities*, edited by Sir H. Ellis, vol. ii. p. 324.]

FIVE score of men, money, and pins,
Six score of all other things.

CLIX.

SEE a pin and pick it up,
All the day you'll have good luck;
See a pin and let it lay,
Bad luck you'll have all the day!

CLX.

A SWARM of bees in May,
Is worth a load of hay;
A swarm of bees in June,
Is worth a silver spoon;
A swarm of bees in July,
Is not worth a fly.

CLXI.

ST. Swithin's day if thou dost rain,
For forty days it will remain.
St. Swithin's day if thou be fair,
For forty days 'twill rain na mair.

CLXII.

To make your candles last for aye,
You wives and maids give ear-o!
To put 'em out 's the only way,
Says honest John Boldero.

CLXIII.

THE taylor of Bisiter,
He has but one eye;
He cannot cut a pair of green galagaskins,
If he were to try.

CLXIV.

NEEDLES and pins, needles and pins,
When a man marries his trouble begins.

CLXV.

RIDDLE me, riddle me, riddle me ree!
None are so blind as those that won't see.

CLXVI.

[ONE version of the following song, which I believe to be the genuine one, is written on the last leaf of MS. Harl. 6580, in a hand of the end of the seventeenth century, but unfortunately it is scarcely adapted for the "ears polite" of modern days. See also MS. Sloane, 406, where it is also quoted.]

A MAN of words and not of deeds
Is like a garden full of weeds;

And when the weeds begin to grow,
It 's like a garden full of snow;
And when the snow begins to fall,
It 's like a bird upon the wall:
And when the bird away does fly,
It 's like an eagle in the sky;
And when the sky begins to roar,
It 's like a lion at the door;
And when the door begins to crack,
It 's like a stick across your back;
And when your back begins to smart,
It 's like a penknife in your heart;
And when your heart begins to bleed,
You're dead, and dead, and dead, indeed.

Sixth Class.—Lullabies.

CLXVII.

Hush a bye, baby, on the tree top,
When the wind blows, the cradle will rock;
When the bough bends, the cradle will fall,
Down will come baby, bough, cradle, and all.

CLXVIII.

Bye, baby bunting,
Daddy 's gone a hunting,
To get a little hare's skin,
To wrap a baby bunting in.

CLXIX.

Hushy baby, my doll, I pray you don't cry,
And I'll give you some bread and some milk by and bye;
Or, perhaps you like custard, or may-be a tart,—
Then to either you're welcome, with all my whole heart.

CLXX.

Bye, O my baby,
When I was a lady,
O then my poor baby didn't cry;
But my baby is weeping,
For want of good keeping,
Oh, I fear my poor baby will die.

CLXXI.

Hush thee, my babby,
Lie still with thy daddy,
Thy mammy has gone to the mill,
To grind thee some wheat,
To make thee some meat,
And so my dear babby lie still.

CLXXII.

Hush a bye á ba lamb,
Hush a bye a milk cow,
You shall have a little stick,
To beat the naughty bow-wow.

CLXXIII.

Cry, baby, cry,
Put your finger in your eye,
And tell your mother it was I.

Seventh Class.—Charms.

CLXXV.

[The three following charms are for the hiccup, and each one must be said thrice in one breath, to render the specific of service.]

When a twister twisting would twist him a twist,
For twisting a twist three twists he will twist;
But if one of the twists untwists from the twist,
The twist untwisting untwists the twist.

CLXXVI.

Robert Rowley rolled a round roll round,
A round roll Robert Rowley rolled round;
Where rolled the round roll Robert Rowley rolled round?

CLXXVII.

Peter Piper picked a peck of pickled pepper;
A peck of pickled pepper Peter Piper picked;
If Peter Piper picked a peck of pickled pepper,
Where is the peck of pickled pepper Peter Piper picked?

CLXXVIII.

[Ady, in his "Candle in the Dark," 4to. Lond. 1655, p. 58, says that this is a charm used for making butter come from the churn. It was to be said thrice.]

Come, butter, come,
Come, butter, come!
Peter stands at the gate,
Waiting for a butter'd cake;
Come, butter, come!

CLXXIX.

I went to the toad that lies under the wall,
I charmed him out, and he came at my call;
I scratch'd out the eyes of the owl before,
I tore the bat's wing, what would you have more?

CLXXX.

[A charm somewhat similar to the following may be seen in the *Townley Mysteries*, p. 91. See a paper in the *Archæologia*, vol. xxvii. p. 253, by the Rev. Launcelot Sharpe, M.A.]

Matthew, Mark, Luke, and John,
Guard the bed that I lay on!
Four corners to my bed,
Four angels round my head!
One to watch, one to pray,
And two to bear my soul away!

CLXXXI.

[The present charm, which appears to be only another version of the one just given, is preserved by Aubrey, in MS. Lansd. 231, fol. 114. It may likewise be found in Ady's "Candle in the Dark," 4to. Lond, 1655, p. 58.]

Matthew, Mark, Luke, and John,
Bless the bed that I lye on!
And blessed guardian-angel, keep
Me safe from danger whilst I sleep!

CLXXXII.

[The following charm was learnt by the late Sir Humphrey Davy, when a boy, as a cure for the cramp.]

Matthew, Mark, Luke, and John, ease us, I beg!
The devil has tied up a knot in my leg.
Crosses three ✠ ✠ ✠ we make to ease us;
Two for the robbers, and one for Christ Jesus.

Eighth Class.—Games.

CLXXXIII.

We are three brethren out of Spain,
Come to court your daughter Jane.
My daughter Jane she is too young,
And has not learn'd her mother-tongue.

Be she young, or be she old,
For her beauty she must be sold.
So fare you well, my lady gay,
We'll call again another day,

Turn back, turn back, thou scornful knight;
And rub thy spurs till they be bright.
Of my spurs take you no thought,
For in this town they were not bought.
So fare you well, my lady gay,
We'll call again another day.

Turn back, turn back, thou scornful knight,
And take the fairest in your sight.
The fairest maid that I can see,
Is pretty Nancy, come to me.

Here comes your daughter safe and sound,
Every pocket with a thousand pound;
Every finger with a gay gold ring;
Please to take your daughter in.

CLXXXIV.

Here we come a piping,
First in spring and then in May,
The queen she sits upon the sand,
Fair as a lilly, white as a wand;
King John has sent you letters three,
And begs you'll read them unto me;
We can't read one, without them all,
So pray Miss Bridget deliver the ball!

CLXXXV.

Sieve my lady's oatmeal,
  Grind my lady's flour,
Put it in a chesnut,
  Let it stand an hour;
One may rush, two may rush,
Come, my girls, walk under the bush.

CLXXXVI.

GIRLS and boys, come out to play,
The moon does shine as bright as day;
Leave your supper and leave your sleep,
And come with your play-fellows into the street.
Come with a whistle, come with a call,
Come with a good will or not at all.
Up the ladder and down the wall,
A halfpenny roll will serve us all.
You find milk, and I'll find flour,
And we'll have a pudding in half an hour.

CLXXXVII.

I WON'T be my father's Jack,
I won't be my mother's Gill,
I will be the fiddler's wife,
And have music when I will.
T'other little tune,
T'other little tune,
Pr'ythee, love, play me
T'other little tune.

CLXXXVIII.

RIDE a cock horse,
To Banbury Cross,
To see what Tommy can buy;

A penny white loaf,
A penny white cake,
And a two-penny apple pie.

CLXXXIX.

SEE saw, Jack in a hedge,
Which is the way to London bridge?
One foot up, and one foot down,
That is the best way to London town.

CXC.

THERE were two black-birds,
Sitting on a hill,
The one nam'd Jack,
The other nam'd Jill;
Fly away Jack!
Fly away Jill!
Come again Jack!
Come again Jill!

CXCI.

TOM Brown's two little Indian boys,
One ran away,
The other wouldn't stay,—
Tom Brown's two little Indian boys.

CXCII.

[The following is a song to a nursery dance.]

Gay go up and gay go down,
To ring the bells of London Town.

Bull's eyes and targets,
Say the bells of St. Marg'ret's.

Brickbats and tiles,
Say the bells of St. Giles.

Halfpence and farthings,
Say the bells of St. Martin's.

Oranges and lemons,
Say the bells of St. Clement's.

Pancakes and fritters,
Say the bells at St. Peter's.

Two sticks and an apple,
Say the bells at Whitechapel.

Old Father Baldpate,
Say the slow bells at Aldgate.

You owe me ten shillings,
Say the bells at St. Helen's.

When will you pay me?
Say the bells at Old Bailey.

When I shall grow rich,
Say the bells at Shoreditch.

Pray, when will that be?
Say the bells at Stepney.

I am sure I don't know,
Says the great bell at Bow.

CXCIII.

SNAIL, snail,
Come out of your hole,
Or else I will beat you
As black as a coal.

CXCIV.

[One child holds a wand to the face of another, repeating these lines, and making grimaces, to cause the latter to laugh, and so to the others; those who laugh paying a forfeit.]

BUFF says Buff to all his men,
And I say Buff to you again;
Buff neither laughs nor smiles,
But carries his face
With a very good grace,
And passes the stick to the very next place!

CXCV.

DANCE, Bumpkin, dance,
(*Keep the thumb in motion.*)
Dance, ye merrymen, every one;
(*All the fingers in motion.*)
For Bumpkin, he can dance alone,
(*The thumb only moving.*)
Bumpkin, he can dance alone. (*Ditto.*)
Dance, Foreman, dance,
(*The first finger moving.*)
Dance ye merrymen every one;
(*The whole moving.*)
But Foreman, he can dance alone,
Foreman, he can dance alone.

And so on with the others—naming the 2d finger *Middleman* —the 3d finger *Ringman*—and the 4th finger *Littleman*. Littleman *cannot* dance alone.

CXCVI.

QUEEN Anne, queen Anne, you sit in the sun,
As fair as a lily, as white as a wand.
I send you three letters, and pray read one,
You must read one, if you can't read all,
So pray, Miss or Master, throw up the ball.

CXCVII.

Ride a cock-horse to Banbury-cross,
To buy little Johnny a galloping-horse:
It trots behind, and it ambles before,
And Johnny shall ride till he can ride no more.

CXCVIII.

Ride a cock-horse to Coventry cross;
To see what Emma can buy;
A penny white cake I'll buy for her sake,
And a twopenny tart or a pie.

CXCIX.

Ride a cock-horse to Banbury cross,
To see an old lady upon a white horse,
Rings on her fingers, bells on her toes,
She will have music wherever she goes.

CC.

To market ride the gentlemen,
So do we, so do we;
Then comes the country clown,
Hobbledy gee, Hobbledy gee!

CCI.

THIS is the key of the kingdom.
In that kingdom there is a city.
In that city there is a town.
In that town there is a street.
In that street there is a lane.
In that lane there is a yard.
In that yard there is a house.
In that house there is a room.
In that room there is a bed.
On that bed there is a basket.
In that basket there are some flowers.
Flowers in the basket, basket in the bed, bed in the room, &c. &c.

CCII.

[Song set to five toes.]

1. LET us go to the wood, says this pig;
2. What to do there? says that pig;
3. To look for my mother, says this pig;
4. What to do with her? says that pig;
5. Kiss her to death, says this pig.

CCIII.

Eggs, butter, cheese, bread,
Stick, stock, stone, dead,
Stick him up, stick him down,
Stick him in the old man's crown.

CCIV.

[I believe the following is only a portion of a dialogue, but I have not been able to recover it.]

Here comes a poor woman from baby-land,
With three small children in her hand:
One can brew, the other can bake,
The other can make a pretty round cake.

CCV.

[A string of children, hand in hand, stand in a row. A child (A) stands in front of them, as leader; two other children (B and C) form an arch, each holding both the hands of the other]

A. Draw a pail of water,
For my lady's daughter;
My father's a king, and my mother's a queen,
My two little sisters are dress'd in green,
Stamping grass and parsley,
Marigold leaves and daisies.

B. One rush, two rush,
Pray thee, fine lady, come under my bush.

[A passes under the arch, followed by the whole string of children, the last of whom is taken captive by B and C. The verses are repeated, until the whole are taken.]

CCVI.

ELEVEN comets in the sky,
Some low and some high;
Nine peacocks in the air,
I wonder how they all came there.
I do not know and I do not care;
Seven lobsters in a dish,
As fresh as any heart could wish;
Six beetles against the wall,
Close by an old woman's apple-stall;
Four horses stuck in a bog,
Three monkeys tied to a clog;
Two pudding-ends would choke a dog,
With a gaping, wide-mouthed, waddling frog.

CCVII.

[A Scotch version of the song already given at p. 109.]

LAZY dukes, that sit in your neuks,
And winna come out to play;

Leave your supper, leave your sleep,
Come out and play at hide-and-seek.
I've a cherry, I've a chess,
I've a bonny blue glass,
I've a dog among the corn,
Blow Willie Buckhorn.
Three score of Highland kye,
One booly-backed,
One blind of an eye,
An' a' the rest hawkit.
Laddie wi' the shelly-coat
Help me owre the ferry-boat;
The ferry-boat is owre dear,
Ten pounds every year.
The fiddler's in the Canongate,
The piper's in the Abbey,
Huzza! cocks and hens,
Flee awa' to your cavey.

CCVIII.

THERE were three jovial Welshmen,
As I have heard them say,
And they would go a-hunting
Upon St. David's day.

All the day they hunted,
And nothing could they find,
But a ship a-sailing,
A-sailing with the wind.

One said it was a ship,
  The other he said, nay;
The third said it was a house,
  And the chimney blown away.

And all the night they hunted,
  And nothing could they find,
But the moon a-gliding,
  A-gliding with the wind.

One said it was the moon,
  The other he said, nay;
The third said it was a cheese,
  And half o't cut away.

CCIX.

[Song set to five fingers.]

1. This little pig went to market;
2. This little pig staid at home;
3. This little pig had a bit of bread and butter;
4. This little pig had none;
5. This little pig said, Wee, wee, wee!
   I can't find my way home.

CCX.

[A game at ball.]

Cucko, cherry tree,
Catch a bird, and give it to me;
Let the tree be high or low,
Let it hail, rain, or snow.

CCXI.

I can make diet bread,
Thick and thin;
I can make diet bread,
Fit for the king.

CCXII.

[The following lines are sung by children when starting for a race.]

Good horses, bad horses,
What is the time of day?
Three o'clock, four o'clock,
Now fare you away.

CCXIII.

[The following is the Oxfordshire version of the game of the Confessional, as shown in shadows on the wall.]

Father, O father, I'm come to confess,
Well, my daughter, well!
Last night I call'd the cat a beast.
Shocking, my daughter, shocking!
What penance? my father, what penance?
What penance! my daughter, what penance!
What penance shall I do?
Kiss me.

CCXIV.

[The Kentish version of the same game.]

Good morning, father Francis.
Good morning, Mrs. Sheckleton. What has brought you abroad so early, Mrs. Sheckleton?
I have come to confess a great sin, father Francis.
What's it, Mrs. Sheckleton?
Your cat stole a pound of my butter, father Francis!
O, no sin at all, Mrs. Sheckleton.
But I kill'd your cat for it, father Francis.
O a very great sin indeed, Mrs. Sheckleton, you must do penance.
What penance, father Francis?
Kiss me.
O no, O yes, O no, O yes, &c. *ad libitum.*

CCXV.

[Children hunting bats.]

BAT, bat *(clap hands)*,
Come under my hat,
And I'll give you a slice of bacon;
And when I bake,
I'll give you a cake,
If I am not mistaken.

CCXVI.

[THIS is acted by two or more girls, who walk or dance up and down, turning, when they say, "turn, cheeses, turn." The "green cheeses," as I am informed, are made with sage and potatoe-tops. Two girls are said to be "cheese and cheese."]

GREEN cheeses, yellow laces,
Up and down the market-places,
Turn, cheeses, turn!

CCXVII.

[Two of the strongest children are selected, A and B. A stands within a ring of the children, B being outside.]

A. Who is going round my sheepfold?
B. Only poor old Jacky Lingo.
A. Don't steal any of my black sheep.

B. No, no more I will, only by one,
Up, says Jacky Lingo. (*Strikes one.*)

[The child struck leaves the ring, and takes hold of B behind; B in the same manner takes the other children, one by one, gradually increasing his tail on each repetition of the verses, until he has got the whole. A then tries to get them back; B runs away with them; they try to shelter themselves behind B; A drags them off, one by one, setting them against a wall, until he has recovered all. A regular tearing game, as children say.]

CCXVIII.

[CHILDREN stand round, and are counted one by one by means of this rhyme, which I have already given in a different form at p. 89. The child upon whom the last number falls is *out*, for "Hide or Seek," or any other game where a victim is required. A cock and bull story of this kind is related of the historian Josephus.]

HICKORY (1), Dickory (2), Dock (3),
The mouse ran up the clock (4),
The clock struck one (5),
The mouse was gone (6);
O (7), U (8), T (9), spells OUT!

CCXIX.

[A number of boys and girls stand round one in the middle, who repeats the following lines, counting the children until one is counted out by the end of the verses.]

RING me (1), ring me (2), ring me rary (3),
As I go round (4), ring by ring (5),

A virgin (6) goes a maying (7),
Here 's a flower (8), and there 's a flower (9),
Growing in my lady's garden (10);
If you set your foot awry (11),
Gentle John will make you cry (12),
If you set your foot amiss (13),
Gentle John (14) will give you a kiss.

[The child upon whom (14) falls, is then taken out and forced to select one of the opposite sex. The middle child then proceeds.]

This [lady or gentleman] is none of ours,
Has put [his or her] self in [the selected child's] power,
So clap all hands, and ring all bells, and make the
wedding o'er. [*All clap hands.*]

[If the child taken by lot joins in the clapping, the selected child is rejected, and, I think, takes the middle place. Otherwise, I think, there is a salute.]

CCXX.

SEE-SAW, sacradown;
Which is the way to London town?
One foot up, and the other down,
And that is the way to London town.
1, 2, 3, 4, 5,
I caught a hare alive;
6, 7, 8, 9, 10,
I let him go again.

CCXXI.

Highty cock O!
To London we go,
To York we ride;
And Edward has pussy-cat tied to his side;
He shall have little dog tied to the other,
And then he goes trid trod to see his grandmother.

CCXXII.

See-saw, jack a daw,
What is a craw to do wi' her;
She has not a stocking to put on her,
And the craw has not one for to gi' her.

CCXXIII.

[Another version of No. 219.]

As I go round ring by ring,
A maiden goes a maying,
And here's a flower and there's a flower,
As red as any daisy. If you set your foot awry,
Gentle John will make you cry;
If you set your foot amiss,
Gentle John will give you a good kiss.

CCXXIV.

One old Oxford ox opening oysters;
Two tee totums totally tired of trying to trot to Tadberry;
Three tall tigers tippling ten-penny tea;
Four fat friars fanning fainting flies;
Five frippy Frenchmen foolishly fishing for flies;
Six sportsmen shooting snipes!
Seven Severn salmons swallowing shrimps;
Eight Englishmen eagerly examining Europe;
Nine nimble noblemen nibbling nonpareils;
Ten tinkers tinkling upon ten tin tinder-boxes with ten tenpenny tacks;
Eleven elephants elegantly equipt;
Twelve typographical topographers typically translating types.

CCXXV.

[A stands with a row of girls (her daughters) behind her; B, a suitor advances.]

B. Trip trap over the grass; If you please will you let one of your [eldest] daughters come,
Come and dance with me?
I will give you pots and pans, I will give you brass,
I will give you anything for a pretty lass.

A says "No."

B. I will give you gold and silver, I will give you pearl,
I will give you anything for a pretty girl.

A. Take one, take one, the fairest you may see.
B. The fairest one that I can see
Is pretty Nancy, come to me.

[B carries one off, and says:]

You shall have a duck, my dear,
And you shall have a drake,
And you shall have a young man apprentice for
your sake.

(Children say:)

If this young man should happen to die,
And leave this poor woman a widow,
The bells shall all ring, and the birds shall all sing,
And we'll all clap hands together.

[So it is repeated until the whole are taken.]

The verses of the Three Knights of Spain are played in nearly the same way.

CCXXVI.

THE first day of Christmas,
My mother sent to me,
A partridge in a pear-tree.
The second day of Christmas,
My mother sent to me,
Two turtle doves and a partridge in a pear-tree.
The third, &c.
Three French hens, two turtle doves, and a partridge, &c.

The fourth, &c.
Four canary birds, three French hens, two turtle, &c.
The fifth, &c.
Five gold rings, &c.
The sixth, &c.
Six geese a laying, &c.
The seventh, &c.
Seven swans a swimming, &c.
The eighth, &c.
Eight ladies dancing, &c.
The ninth, &c.
Nine lords a leaping, &c.
The tenth, &c.
Ten ships a sailing, &c.
The eleventh, &c.
Eleven ladies spinning, &c.
The twelfth, &c.
Twelve bells ringing, &c.

[Each child in succession repeats the gifts of the day, and forfeits for each mistake. This accumulative process is a favourite with children; in early writers, such as Homer, the repetition of messages, &c. pleases on the same principle.]

Ninth Class.—Paradoxes.

CCXXVII.

O THAT I was where I would be,
Then would I be where I am not;
But where I am I must be,
And where I would be I can not.

CCXXVIII.

HERE am I, little jumping Joan;
When nobody's with me,
I'm always alone.

CCLXXIX.

[The conclusion of the following resembles a verse in the nursery history of Mother Hubbard.]

THERE was an old woman and what do you think?
She lived upon nothing but victuals and drink.
Victuals and drink were the chief of her diet,
And yet this old woman could never be quiet.

K

She went to the baker, to buy her some bread,
And when she came home, her old husband was dead;
She went to the clerk to toll the bell,
And when she came back her old husband was well.

CCXXX.

THE rule of the road is a paradox quite,
And custom has prov'd it so long:
He that goes to the left is sure to go right,
And he that goes right must go wrong.

CCXXXI.

[The following is quoted in Parkins' Reply to Dr. Stukeley's second number of *Origines Roystonianæ*, 4to. Lond. 1748, p. 6.]

PETER White will ne'er go right,
And would you know the reason why?
He follows his nose where'er he goes,
And that stands all awry.

Tenth Class.—Literal.

CCXXXII.

A, B, C, tumble down dee,
The cat's in the cupboard, and can't see me.

CCXXXIII.

1, 2, 3, 4, 5,
I caught a hare alive;
6, 7, 8, 9, 10,
I let her go again.

CCXXXIV.

GREAT A, little a,
Bouncing B,
The cat's in the cupboard,
And she can't see.

CCXXXV.

ONE, two,
Buckle my shoe;
Three, four,
Shut the door;
Five, six,
Pick up sticks;
Seven, eight,
Lay them straight;
Nine, ten,
A good fat hen;
Eleven, twelve,
Who will delve?
Thirteen, fourteen,
Maids a courting;
Fifteen, sixteen,
Maids a kissing;
Seventeen, eighteen,
Maids a waiting;
Nineteen, twenty,
My stomach's empty.

CCXXXVI.

PAT-a-cake, pat-a cake, baker's man:
So I will master as fast as I can:
Pat it, and prick it, and mark it with T,
Put in the oven for Tommy and me.

CCXXXVII.

[The following is taken from MS. Sloan. 2497, of the sixteenth century.]

N. for a word of deniance,
E. with a figure fiftie,
Spelleth his name that newer
Will be thriftie.

CCXXXVIII.

Miss one two and three, could never agree,
While they gossiped round a tea caddy.

CCXXXIX.

One's none;
Two's some;
Three's a many;
Four's a penny.
Five is a little hundred.

Eleventh Class.—Scholastic.

CCXL.

A DILLER, a doller,
A ten o'clock scholar,
What makes you come so soon?
You us'd to come at ten o'clock,
And now you come at noon.

CCXLI.

MISTRESS Mary, quite contrary,
How does your garden grow?
With cockle shells, and silver bells,
And cowslips all a row.

CCXLII.

Donkey walks on four legs,
And I walk on two;
The last I saw,
Was very like you.

CCXLIII.

Liar, liar, lick spit,
Turn about the candlestick.
What's good for liar?
Brimstone and fire.

CCXLIV.

When I was a little boy my mammy kept me in,
But now I am a great boy I'm fit to serve the king;
I can hand a musket, and I can smoke a pipe,
And I can kiss a pretty girl at twelve o'clock at night.

CCXLV.

Tell tale, tit!
Your tongue shall be slit,
And all the dogs in the town
Shall have a little bit.

CCXLVI.

Multiplication is vexation,
Division is as bad;
The rule of three does puzzle me,
And practice drives me mad,

Twelfth Class.—Customs.*

CCXLVII.

[The following is sung at the Christmas mummings in Somersetshire.]

Here comes I,
  Liddle man Jan,
Wi my ȝword
  In my han!

If you don't all do,
  As you be told by I,
I'll ȝend you all to York,
  Vor to make apple-pie.

CCXLVIII.

Dibbity, dibbity, dibbity, doe,
Give me a pan-cake
    And I'll go.
Dibbity, dibbity, dibbity, ditter,
Please to give me
    A bit of a fritter.

* This class might be extended to great length, but I shall content myself with giving a few, and referring to Sir H. Ellis's edition of Brand's Popular Antiquities for more.

CCXLIX.

[It was probably the custom, on repeating these lines, to hold the snail to a candle, in order to make it quit the shell. In Normandy it was the practice at Christmas for boys to run round fruit trees, with lighted torches, singing these lines:

Taupes et mulots,
Sortez de vos clos,
Sinon vous brulerai et la barbe et les os.]

Snail, snail, come out of your hole,
Or else I'll beat you as black as a coal.

CCL.

I see the moon, and the moon sees me,
God bless the moon, and God bless me.

CCLI.

[Aubrey, in his "Remaines of Gentilisme and Judaisme," gives another version of this song, as current in the seventeenth century, very curious, but unfortunately much too indelicate to be printed in a book emanating from the Percy Society, or indeed any other.]

When I was a little girl,
I wash'd my mother's dishes;
I put my finger in my eye,
And pull'd out little fishes.

CCLII.

Herrings, herrings, white and red,
Ten a penny, Lent's dead.
Rise dame and give an egg,
Or else a piece of bacon.
One for Peter, two for Paul,
Three for Jack a Lent's all,
Away, Lent, away.

CCLIII.

[The unmarried ladies in the north address the new moon in the following lines :]

All hail to the moon! all hail to thee!
I prithee, good moon, declare to me
This night who my husband must be!

Thirteenth Class.—Songs.

CCLIV.

Parson Darby wore a black gown,
And every button cost half a crowu;
From port to port, and toe to toe,
Turn the ship and away we go!

CCLV.

I had a little pony,
  His name was Dapple-grey,
I lent him to a lady,
  To ride a mile away;
She whipped him, she slashed him,
  She rode him through the mire;
I would not lend my pony now
  For all the lady's hire.

CCLVI.

As Tommy Snooks, and Bessy Brooks,
  Were walking out one Sunday,
Says Tommy Snooks to Bessy Brooks,
  "Tomorrow will be Monday."

CCLVII.

[A north-country song.]

SAYS t'auld man tit oak tree,
Young and lusty was I when I kenn'd thee;
I was young and lusty, I was fair and clear,
Young and lusty was I mony a lang year,
But sair fail'd am I, sair fail'd now,
Sair fail'd am I sen I kenn'd thou.

CCLVIII.

[The following song is given in Whiter's *Specimen of a Commentary on Shakespeare*, 8vo. Lond. 1794, p. 19, as peculiar to Cambridge and Norfolk.]

HEIGH, ho! heigh, ho!
Dame what makes your ducks to die?
What a pize ails 'em, what a pize ails 'em?
Heigh, ho! heigh, ho!
Dame, what ails your ducks to die?
Eating o' polly wigs, eating o' polly wigs. [i. e. Tadpoles.]
Heigh, ho! heigh, ho!

CCLIX.

Buz, quoth the blue fly,
  Hum, quoth the bee,
Buz and hum they cry,
  And so do we:
In his ear, in his nose,
  Thus, do you see;
He ate the dormouse,
  Else it was thee.

CCLX.

[Out of the many songs relating to the heroine of the following stanza, one only has been deemed eligible for insertion in this volume.]

NANCY DAWSON was so fine,
She wouldn't get up to serve the swine,
She lies in bed till eight or nine,
So its oh! poor Nancy Dawson.

CCLXI.

WE'RE all dry with drinking on't,
We're all dry with drinking on't;
The piper kiss'd the fiddler's wife,
And I can't sleep for thinking on't.

CCXLII.

THERE was an old man who liv'd in Middle Row,
He had five hens, and a name for them, oh!
Bill and Ned and Battock,
Cut-her-foot and Pattock,
Chuck, my lady Prattock,
Go to thy nest and lay.

CCLXIII.

WHO comes here?
A grenadier.
What do you want?
A pot of beer.
Where is your money?
I've forgot.
Get you gone,
You drunken sot.

CCLXIV.

CURLY locks! curly locks! wilt thou be mine?
Thou shalt not wash dishes, nor yet feed the swine:
But sit on a cushion, and sew a fine seam,
And feed upon strawberries, sugar, and cream!

CCLXV.

I'LL sing you a song,
Nine verses long,
    For a pin;
Three and three are six,
And three are nine;
You are a fool,
    And the pin is mine.

CCLXVI.

THE quaker's wife got up to bake,
  Her children all about her,
She gave them every one a cake,
  And the miller wants his moulter.

CCLXVII.

BARBER, barber, shave a pig,
How many hairs will make a wig?
"Four and twenty, that's enough."
Give the poor barber a pinch of snuff.

CCLXVIII.

We'll go a shooting, says Robin to Bobbin;
We'll go a shooting, says Richard to Robin;
We'll go a shooting, says John all alone;
We'll go a shooting, says every one.

What shall we kill, says Robin to Bobbin;
What shall we kill, says Richard to Robin;
What shall we kill, says John all alone;
What shall we kill, says every one.

We'll shoot at that wren, says Robin to Bobbin;
We'll shoot at that wren, says Richard to Robin;
We'll shoot at that wren, says John all alone;
We'll shoot at that wren, says every one.

She's down, she's down, says Robin to Bobbin;
She's down, she's down, says Richard to Robin;
She's down, she's down, says John all alone;
She's down, she's down, says every one.

How shall we get her home, says Robin to Bobbin;
How shall we get her home, says Richard to Robin;
How shall we get her home, says John all alone;
How shall we get her home, says every one.

We'll hire a cart, says Robin to Bobbin;
We'll hire a cart, says Richard to Robin;
We'll hire a cart, says John all alone;
We'll hire a cart, says every one.

Then hoist, boys, hoist, says Robin to Bobbin;
Then hoist, boys, hoist, says Richard to Robin;
Then hoist, boys, hoist, says John all alone;
Then hoist, boys, hoist, says every one.

So they brought her away, after each pluck'd a feather,
And when they got home, shar'd the booty together.

CCLXIX.

Up hill and down dale;
Butter is made in every vale;
And if that Nancy Cock
Is a good girl,
She shall have a spouse,
And make butter anon,
Before her old grandmother
Grows a young man.

CCLXX.

As I was going up Pippen-hill
Pippen-hill was dirty,
There I met a pretty miss,
And she dropt me a curtesy.

Little miss, pretty miss,
Blessings light upon you,
If I had half-a-crown a day,
I'd spend it all upon you.

CCLXXI.

I am a pretty wench,
And I come a great way hence,
And sweethearts I can get none:
But every dirty sow,
Can get sweethearts enow,
And I, pretty wench, can get never a one.

CCLXXII.

There was a little boy and a little girl
Liv'd in an alley;
Says the little boy to the little girl,
Shall I, oh, shall I?

Says the little girl to the little boy,
What shall we do?
Says the little boy to the little girl,
I will kiss you.

CCLXXIII.

Trip upon trenchers, and dance upon dishes,
My mother sent me for some barm, some barm;
She bid me tread lightly, and come again quickly,
For fear the young men should do me some harm.

Yet didn't you see, yet didn't you see,
What naughty tricks they put upon me:
They broke my pitcher,
And spilt the water,
And huff'd my mother,
And chid her daughter,
And kiss'd my sister instead of me.

CCLXXIV.

I'll sing you a song:
The days are long,
The woodcock and the sparrow:
The little dog has burnt his tail,
And he must be hang'd to-morrow.

CCLXXV.

The cat sat asleep by the side of the fire,
The mistress snored loud as a pig:
Jack took up his fiddle, by Jenny's desire,
And struck up a bit of a jig.

CCLXXVI.

The sow came in with the saddle,
The little pig rock'd the cradle,
The dish jump'd over the table,
To see the pot with the ladle.
The broom behind the butt
Call'd the dish-clout a nasty slut:
Odds-bobs, says the gridiron, can't you agree?
I'm the head constable,—come along with me.

CCLXXVII.

Around the green gravel the grass grows green,
And all the pretty maids are plain to be seen;
Wash them with milk, and clothe them with silk,
And write their names with a pen and ink.

CCLXXVIII.

[The song of a boy while passing his hour of solitude in a corn-field.]

Awa' birds, away,
Take a little and leave a little,
And do not come again;
For if you do,
I will shoot you through,
And there is an end of you.

CCLXXIX.

THOMAS a Didymus, king of the Jews,
Jumped into the fire and burned both his shoes.

CCLXXX.

WHAT care I how black I be,
Twenty pounds will marry me;
If twenty won't, forty shall,
I am my mother's bouncing girl.

CCLXXXI.

A LITTLE old man and I fell out;
How shall we bring this matter about?
Bring it about as well as you can,
Get you gone, you little old man!

CCLXXXII.

BOBBY SHAFT is gone to sea,
With silver buckles at his knee;
When he'll come home he'll marry me,
Pretty Bobby Shaft!

Bobby Shaft is fat and fair,
Combing down his yellow hair;
He's my love for evermore!
Pretty Bobby Shaft!

CCLXXXIII.

RIDE, baby, ride,
Pretty baby shall ride,
And have little puppy-dog tied to her side,
And little pussy-cat tied to the other,
And away she shall ride to see her grandmother.
To see her grandmother,
To see her grandmother.

CCLXXXIV.

THE rose is red, the violet's blue,
The honey's sweet, and so are you.
Thou art my love, and I am thine;
I drew thee to my Valentine;
The lot was cast, and then I drew,
And fortune said it should be you.

CCLXXXV.

ONE misty moisty morning,
When cloudy was the weather,
There I met an old man
Clothed all in leather;
Clothed all in leather,
With cap under his chin.
How do you do, and how do you do,
And how do you do again?

CCLXXXVI.

I LOVE sixpence, pretty little sixpence,
  I love sixpence better than my life.
I spent a penny of it, I spent another,
  And took fourpence home to my wife.

Oh, my little fourpence, pretty little fourpence,
  I love fourpence better than my life;
I spent a penny of it, I spent another,
  And I took twopence home to my wife.

Oh, my little twopence, my pretty little twopence,
  I love twopence better than my life;
I spent a penny of it, I spent another,
  And I took nothing home to my wife.

Oh, my little nothing, my pretty little nothing,
  What will nothing buy for my wife?
I have nothing, I spend nothing,
  I love nothing better than my wife.

CCLXXXVII.

OF all the gay birds that e'er I did see,
The owl is the fairest by far to me;
For all the day long she sits on a tree,
And when the night comes away flies she.

CCLXXXVIII.

I HAD a little hobby-horse, and it was well shod,
It carried me to the mill-door, trod, trod, trod;
When I got there I gave a great shout,
Down came the hobby-horse, and I cried out.
Fie upon the miller, he was a great beast,
He would not come to my house, I made a little feast;
I had but little, but I would give him some,
For playing of his bagpipes and beating his drum.

CCLXXXIX.

DANCE, little baby, dance up high,
  Never mind, baby, mother is by;
Crow and caper, caper and crow,
  There, little baby, there you go;
Up to the ceiling, down to the ground,
  Backwards and forwards, round and round;
Dance, little baby, and mother will sing,
  With the merry coral, ding, ding, ding.

CCXC.

IF all the seas were one sea,
What a *great* sea would that be!
And if all the trees were one tree,
What a *great* tree that would be!

And if all the axes were one axe,
What a *great* axe that would be!
And if all the men were one man,
What a *great* man he would be!
And if the *great* man took the *great* axe,
And cut down the *great* tree,
And let it fall into the *great* sea,
What a splish splash *that* would be!!

CCXCI.

John Ball shot them all;
John Scott made the shot,
  But John Ball shot them all.

John Wyming made the priming,
And John Brammer made the rammer,
And John Scott made the shot,
  But John Ball shot them all.

John Block made the stock,
And John Brammer made the rammer,
And John Wyming made the priming,
And John Scott made the shot,
  But John Ball shot them all.

John Crowder made the powder,
And John Block made the stock,

And John Wyming made the priming,
And John Brammer made the rammer,
And John Scott made the shot,
But John Ball shot them all.

John Puzzle made the muzzle,
And John Crowder made the powder,
And John Block made the stock,
And John Wyming made the priming,
And John Brammer made the rammer,
And John Scott made the shot,
But John Ball shot them all.

John Clint made the flint,
And John Puzzle made the muzzle,
And John Crowder made the powder,
And John Block made the stock,
And John Wyming made the priming,
And John Brammer made the rammer,
And John Scott made the shot,
But John Ball shot them all.

John Patch made the match,
John Clint made the flint,
John Puzzle made the muzzle,
John Crowder made the powder,
John Block made the stock,
John Wyming made the priming,
John Brammer made the rammer,
John Scott made the shot,
But John Ball shot them all.

CCXCII.

LITTLE Tommy Tacket,
    Sits upon his cracket;*
Half a yard of cloth will make him coat and jacket;
    Make him coat and jacket,
    Breeches to the knee.
And if you will not have him, you may let him be.

---

* A little three-legged stool seen by the ingle of every cottage in the north of England.

Fourteenth Class.—Fragments.

CCXCIII.

LITTLE boy, pretty boy, where was you born?
In Lincolnshire, master: come blow the cow's horn.
A half-penny pudding, a penny pie,
A shoulder of mutton, and that love I.

CCXCIV.

WHEN I was a little boy, I had but little wit,
It is some time ago and I've no more yet;
Nor ever ever shall, until that I die,
For the longer I live, the more fool am I.

CCXCV.

Cross patch,
Draw the latch,
Sit by the fire and spin;
Take a cup,
And drink it up,
And call your neighbours in.

CCXCVI

Rock-a-bye, baby, the cradle is green;
Father's a nobleman, mother's a queen;
And Betty's a lady, and wears a gold ring;
And Johnny's a drummer, and drums for the king.

CCXCVII.

Shake a leg, wag a leg, when will you gang?
At midsummer, mother, when the days are lang.

CCXCVIII.

How many miles is it to Babylon?
Threescore miles and ten.
Can I get there by candle-light?
Yes, and back again,
If your heels are nimble and light,
You may get there by candle-light.

CCXCIX.

[The following stanza is of very considerable antiquity, and is common in Yorkshire. See Hunter's Hallamshire Glossary, p. 56.]

Lady-cow, lady-cow, fly thy way home,
Thy house is on fire, thy children all gone,
All but one that ligs under a stone,
Ply thee home, lady-cow, ere it be gone.

CCC.

Sing jigmijole, the pudding-bowl,
The table and the frame;
My master he did cudgel me,
For kissing of my dame.

NOTES.

P. 1, l. 1. *When Good King Arthur.* There is a similar song on king Stephen, which is introduced in an old play; but this is the genuine one recorded in the nursery.

P. 2, l. 16. *The house that Jack built.* The Hebrew tale which I have given, may possibly be the original of all accumulative stories of the same kind. The tale of the old woman and the crooked sixpence is one of this class, and I here insert two versions of it:

"An old woman was sweeping her house, and she found a little crooked sixpence. What, said she, shall I do with this little sixpence? I will go to market, and buy a little pig. As she was coming home, she came to a style: but piggy would not go over the stile.

"She went a little further, and she met a dog. So she said to the dog, Dog! bite pig; piggy won't go over the stile; and I shan't get home to night. But the dog would not.

"She went a little further, and she met a stick. So she said, Stick! stick! beat dog; dog won't bite pig; piggy won't get over the stile; and I shan't get home to night. But the stick would not.

"She went a little further, and she met a fire. So she said, Fire! fire! burn stick; stick won't beat dog; dog won't bite pig; (*and so forth, always repeating the foregoing words.*) But the fire would not.

"She went a little further; and she met some water. So she said, Water! water! quench fire: fire won't burn stick. But the water would not.

"She went a little further, and she met an ox. So she said, Ox! ox! drink water, water won't quench fire, &c. But the ox would not.

"She went a little further, and she met a butcher. So she said, Butcher! butcher! kill ox; ox won't drink water, &c. But the butcher would not.

"She went a little further, and she met a rope. So she said, Rope! rope! hang butcher! butcher won't kill ox, &c. But the rope would not.

"She went a little further, and she met a rat. So she said, Rat! rat! gnaw rope; rope won't hang butcher, &c. But the rat would not.

"She went a little further, and she met a cat. So she said, Cat! cat, kill rat; rat won't gnaw rope, &c. But the cat said, to her, If you will go to yonder cow, and fetch me a saucer of milk; I will kill the rat. So away went the old woman to the cow.

"But the cow said to her, If you will go to yonder haystack,* and fetch me a handful of hay; I'll give you the milk. So away went the old woman to the haystack; and she brought the hay to the cow.

"As soon as the cow had eaten the hay, she gave the old woman the milk; and away she went with it in a saucer to the cat.

"As soon as the cat had lapped up the milk, the cat began to kill the rat; the rat began to gnaw the rope; the rope began to hang the butcher; the butcher began to kill the ox; the ox began to drink the water; the water began to quench the fire; the fire began to burn the stick; the stick began to beat the dog; the dog began to bite the pig; the little pig in a fright jumped over the stile; and so the old woman got home that night."

"There was an old woman, that lived in a house: and, sweeping under her bed, she found a silver penny. So she went to

---

* Or, haymakers, proceeding thus in the stead of the rest of this paragraph:—"and fetch me a wisp of hay, I'll give you the milk. So away the old woman went, but the haymakers said to her, If you will go to yonder stream, and fetch us a bucket of water, we'll give you the hay. So away the old woman went, but when she got to the stream, she found the bucket was full of holes. So she covered the bottom with pebbles, and then filled the bucket with water, and away she went back with it to the haymakers; and they gave her a wisp of hay."

market and bought a pig: but as she came home, the pig would not go over the stile.

"She went a little further, and she met a dog; and she said to the dog, Good dog! bite pig: pig won't go; and it's time that I was at home an hour and a half ago. But the dog would not. (*And so forth, as in the other story, mutatis mutandis, to the Rat.*)

"She went a little further, and she met a cat. So she said to the cat, Good cat! kill rat; rat won't bite rope; rope won't hang butcher; butcher won't kill ox; ox won't drink water; water won't quench fire; fire won't burn stick; stick won't beat pig; pig won't go. And it's time that I was at home an hour and a half ago.

"The cat began to kill the rat; the rat began (*and so forth, as in the other story*;) the pig began to go. And so the old woman got home at last."

It will be observed that these two versions, for which I am indebted to Mr. Black, are much more like the Hebrew tale than *The House that Jack built;* but as our collection would scarcely be complete without this latter, I shall insert a copy of it:

1. THIS is the house that Jack built.

2. This is the malt,
That lay in the house that Jack built.

3. This is the rat,
That ate the malt,
That lay in the house that Jack built.

4. This is the cat,
That kill'd the rat,
That ate the malt,
That lay in the house that Jack built.

5. This is the dog,
That worried the cat,
That kill'd the rat,
That ate the malt,
That lay in the house that Jack built.

6. This is the cow with the crumpled horn,
That tossed the dog,

That worried the cat,
That kill'd the rat,
That ate the malt,
That lay in the house that Jack built.

7. This is the maiden all forlorn,
That milk'd the cow with the crumpled horn,
That tossed the dog,
That worried the cat,
That killed the rat,
That ate the malt,
That lay in the house that Jack built.

8. This is the man all tatter'd and torn,
That kissed the maiden all forlorn,
That milk'd the cow with the crumpled horn,
That tossed the dog,
That worried the cat,
That killed the rat,
That ate the malt,
That lay in the house that Jack built.

9. This is the priest all shaven and shorn,
That married the man all tatter'd and torn,
That kissed the maiden all forlorn,
That milk'd the cow with the crumpled horn,
That tossed the dog,
That worried the cat,
That killed the rat,
That ate the malt,
That lay in the house that Jack built.

10. This is the cock that crow'd in the morn,
That wak'd the priest all shaven and shorn,
That married the man all tatter'd and torn,
That kissed the maiden all forlorn,
That milk'd the cow with the crumpled horn,
That tossed the dog,
That worried the cat,
That killed the rat,
That ate the malt,
That lay in the house that Jack built.

11. This is the farmer sowing his corn,
That kept the cock that crow'd in the morn,
That wak'd the priest all shaven and shorn,
That married the man all tatter'd and torn,
That kissed the maiden all forlorn,
That milk'd the cow with the crumpled horn.
That tossed the dog,
That worried the cat,
That killed the rat,
That ate the malt,
That lay in the house that Jack built.

P. 9, l. 10. *The rose is red.* The tune to this may be found in the "English Dancing Master," 1650.

P. 11, l. 5. *Little.* Sometimes, *pretty.*

P. 11, l. 12. *To gern.* That is, to cry as a child.

P. 12, l. 1. *The king of France.* In a little tract, called "The Pigges Corantoe, or Newes from the North," 4to. Lond. 1642, this is called "Old Tarlton's Song." This fact is mentioned in Mr. Collier's *Hist. Dram. Poet.* vol. ii. p. 352, and also in the preface to Mr. Wright's *Political Ballads*, printed for the Percy Society. It is perhaps a parody on the popular epigram on Jack and Jill:

"Jack and Jill went up the hill,
To fetch a pail of water;
Jack fell down, and broke his crown,
And Jill came tumbling after."

There was an old play, now lost, called "Jack and Jill." I may here take the opportunity of inserting the following, which was accidentally omitted in the historical class:

"High diddle ding!
Did you hear the bells ring?
The parliament soldiers are gone to the king.
Some they did laugh, some they did cry,
To see the parliament soldiers pass by."

P. 13, l. 7. *There was a man in Thessaly.* Sometimes, "There dwelt a man in Babylon," and is so quoted in "Twelfth Night," act ii. scene 3.

P. 14, l. 8. *Deuce take the.* Sometimes, "down came."

P. 16, l. 9. *There was a little man.* Sung to the same tune as No. 52. The following version is taken from a broad-side printed at Strawberry Hill in the last century:

"There was a little man, and he woo'd a little maid,
And he said, my little maid, will you wed?
I have little more to say, than will you yea or nay?
For little said is soon mended.

"Then this little maid she said, little sir, you've little said,
To induce a little maid for to wed;
You must say a little more, and must add a little dower,
E'er I make a little print in your bed.

"Then this little man reply'd, if you'll be my little bride,
I'll raise my love note a little higher;
Tho' I little love to prate, yet you'll find my heart is great,
With the little God of Love all on fire.

"Then the little maid she said, your fire may warm the bed,
But what shall we do for to eat?
Will the flames you're only rich in, make a fire in the kitchen,
And the Little God of Love turn the spit?

"Then this little man he sigh'd, and some say a little cry'd,
And his little heart was big all with sorrow;
I'll be your little slave, and if the little that I have
Be too little, little dear, I will borrow.

"Then this little man so shent, made the little maid relent,
And set her little soul a-thinking;
Tho' his little was but small, yet she had his little all,
And could have of a cat but her skin."

P. 17, l. 1. *I had a little moppet.* This is a game.

P. 19, l. 8. *Three children sliding on the ice.* Sung to the tune of Chevy Chace.

P. 19, l. 18. *Some Christian people.* Music in D'Urfey's "Pills to purge Melancholy." Alluded to in Gay's *Trivia.*

P. 25, l. 5. *There was an old woman.* The first two lines are the same with those of a song in D'Urfey's "Pills to purge Melancholy."

P. 25, l. 15. *Kyloe.* Query, *Kerry.*

P. 26, l. 10. *MS. Lansd.* The reference to this MS. should be No. 762. See "Reliq. Antiq." vol. i. p. 288. A broadside of this states that it is "sung to the tune of the London Prentice."

P. 28, l. 14. *Faustus.* Perhaps Foster.

P. 36, l. 1. *Lucy Locket.* Lucy Locket and Kitty Fisher were two celebrated courtezans of the time of Charles II.

P. 36, l. 13. *Bessy Bell and Mary Gray.* These two stanzas are founded on the well-known Scotch story.

P. 38, l. 13. The merriment of *Jack Horner* has, I believe, long since departed from the modern series, and I therefore give the following copy of it from Douce's collection: "The History of Jack Horner, containing the witty pranks he play'd, from his youth to his riper years, being pleasant for Winter Evenings."

I.

Of his birth and education.

JACK HORNER was a pretty lad,
 near London he did dwell,
His father's heart he made full glad,
 his mother loved him well;

She often sat him on her lap,
  to turn him dry beneath,
And fed him with sweet sugar-pap,
  because he had no teeth.

While little Jack was sweet and young,
  if he by chance should cry,
His mother pretty sonnets sung,
  with lulla-baby-by.

A pretty boy, a curious wit,
  all people spoke his praise,
And in the corner he would sit,
  on Christmas holidays.

And said, Jack Horner in the corner,
  eats good Christmas pye:
With his thumbs pulls out the plums,
  crying what a good boy was I.

These pretty verses which he made
  upon his Christmas cheer,
Did gain him love, as it is said,
  of all both far and near;

For lasses lov'd his company,
  each day above another;
For why? they knew that he would be
  a man before his mother.

He grew, I say, at any rate
  both proper, straight, and trim,
So that young Nancy, Sue, and Kate,
  were all in love with him.

Happy was she that could enjoy
  from him one kind embrace;
Though once he was a little boy,
  yet now he grows apace.

So few were like him far and near,
  and match for him was none;
As being thirteen inches high,
  a giant to Tom Thumb.

Whene'er he took a sword in hand,
  he made his foes to bleed,
As you shall come to understand,
  when you this story read.

II.

Jack frights a tailor for cabbaging cloath out of his coat.

Jack being twenty years of age,
  liv'd with a worthy knight.
In manner of a pretty page,
  to yield him much delight:

The knight right generous and free,
  did for a taylor send,
For to make Jack a livery,
  so much he was his friend,

Of half a yard of good broad cloth
  the coat was to be made,
But yet the taylor he was loth
  to quit his thievish trade.

The knavish taylor was to blame,
  (a crafty cunning wag,)
Be pinch'd as much out of the same
  as made a marble bag.

His coat was spoil'd then being made,
  it came not to his knee:
Jack in a raging passion said,
  I'll be revenged on thee.

The knight he having kill'd a goat,
  whose skin was full as black
I do declare as any soot;
  this project pleased Jack.

He wrapt it round him like a gown
  at twelve o'clock at night,
And then he rambled thro' the town,
  this taylor to affright.

He through a window did advance,
  near to the taylor's bed;
And round the room did skip and dance
  with horns upon his head.

He growl'd and grumbled like a bear,
  and did such anticks play;
As made the taylor then to stare,
  and tremble where he lay.

Seeing the horns hang o'er his head,
  his body short and thick,
The taylor said, speak who art thou?
  quoth Jack, thy friend old Nick:

Thou hast obey'd my order well
  I find in each degree:
And therefore in my gloomy cell,
  I have a place for thee.

For you have been a friend indeed,
  I such a taylor lack:
Therefore come away with speed,
  I'll bear thee on my back:

Sweet Mr. Devil then he cry'd,
  O pardon me I pray;
I can't, I won't, he then reply'd,
  make haste and come away.

The taylor naked to the skin,
  his bed he did refrain,
And down the town thro' thick and thin,
  he ran with might and main.

III.

How he served the cook-maid, who broke his head with a ladle, for making a sop in the dripping-pan.

Another pleasant prank he play'd,
  upon a holiday,
Unto his master's servant maid,
  which was a bloody fray.

Now she was lusty Jane by name,
  and was their constant cook :
And when he to the kitchen came,
  she would him overlook.

Upon a certain day young Jack,
  a slice of bread did take,
And threw it in the dripping-pan,
  that he a sop might make.

So soon as she the same did see,
  it put her in a rage,
And with the basting ladle she
  Jack Horner did engage.

She gave him cracks upon the crown,
  so hard and struck so fast,
That he at length did tumble down,
  and gasping at the last.

But though he did at first retreat,
  he soon returned again ;
For standing fast upon his feet,
  he fought with might and main.

He was but thirteen inches high,
  and she full six times more,
Yet, by his ingenuity,
  he brought her to the floor.

So cruel hard he made her roar,
  she cry'd, Let me alone,
And I will ne'er offend thee more,
  Jack, while my name is Joan.

Why, then, said Jack, if it be so,
that you'll not me offend,
I will this minute let you go,
and so the fray did end.

IV.

An old hermit gives Jack an invisible coat and a pair of enchanted pipes, with which he plays many tricks.

Upon a pleasant holiday,
Jack, going to a fair,
And as he pass'd along the way,
he saw a wonder there;

An aged man sat in a cave,
that could not stand nor go,
His head wore blossoms of the grave,
And look'd as white as snow;

He call'd to Jack, aud this did say,
come hither lad to me,
And if thou dost my will obey,
rewarded thou shalt be;

Bring me a fairing from the town,
at thy own proper cost,
A jug of nappy liquor brown,
thy labour shan't be lost.

Jack made the hermit this reply,
who then sat in the cell,
What's your request I'll not deny,
and so old dad farewell.

At night he being stout and strong
this lad he did not fail,
But at his back lugged along
a swinging jug of ale:

Which when the hermit he beheld,
  it pleas'd him to the heart,
Out of the same a cup he fill'd,
  and said before we part,

I have a pipe which I'll bestow
  upon you,—never doubt,
Whoever hears the same you blow,
  shall dance and skip about;

I have a coat for thee likewise,
  invisible I mean;
And it shall so bedim their eyes,
  that thou shalt not be seen:

If thou should with an hundred meet
  when thus you pass along,
Although upon the open street,
  not one of all the throng

Shall ever see you in the least,
  but hear the music sound;
And wonder that both man and beast
  is forc'd to dance around.

Jack took the coat and bag-pipes too,
  and thankfully did say,
Old Father I will call on you,
  whene'er I come this way.

V.

Of his making six fiddlers dance over hedge and ditch, till they broke all their glasses and crowds.

This coat and pipe he having got,
  he homewards trudg'd with speed;
At length it was his happy lot
  to cross a pleasant mead;

Where he six fidlers soon espy'd
  returning from the fair;
Under their coats crowds by their sides,
  with many others there.

Jack presently his coat put on,
that screen'd him from their sight,
Saying I'll do the best I can
to plague them all this night;

His pipes he straight began to play,
the crowders they did dance;
The tradesmen too, as fast as they,
did caper, skip and prance.

Still he play'd up a merry strain
on his pipes loud and shrill,
So they danc'd and jump'd amain,
tho' sore against their will.

Said they this is enchanted ground,
for though no soul we see,
Yet still the music's pleasant sound,
makes us dance veh'mently.

Jack Horner danc'd and piping went,
straight down into the hollow,
So all these dancers by consent,
they after him did follow.

He led them on thro' bogs and sloughs,
nay, likewise ponds and ditches,
And in the thorny briary boughs,
poor rogues, they tore their breeches!

At last it being somewhat late,
Jack did his piping leave,
So ceas'd, seeing their wretched state
which made them sigh and grieve.

Sure this same is old Nick, I know,
the author of this evil:
And others cry'd if it be so,
he is a merry devil.

Jack Horner laugh'd and went away,
and left them in despair:
So ever since that very day,
no crowders would come there.

VI.

Jack's kindness to the innkeeper, who he puts in a way to pay his debts.

An honest man, an innkeeper
  a friend to honest Jack,
Who was in debt alas! so far
  that he was like to crack;

Now this man had a handsome wife,
  sweet, fair, and beauteous too,—
A Quaker lov'd her as his life,
  And this Jack Horner knew.

The Quaker was an esquire born,
  and did in wealth abound:
Said he, I'll catch him in the corn,
  and put him in the pond.

First to the innkeeper I'll go,
  and when I do him find,
He soon shall understand and know
  that I'll be true and kind.

He met him in a narrow lane,
  and said, my friend, good morrow.
But the innkeeper reply'd again,
  my heart is full of sorrow;

Two hundred pounds I am in debt,
  which I must pay next week,
It makes me sigh, lament, and fret,
  having the coin to seek.

Quoth Jack, if you'll be rul'd by me
  I'll put you in a way,
How you yourself from debts may free
  and all the money pay.

Nay, this is joyful news he cry'd,
  thou art a friend indeed,
Thy wit shall be my rule and guide
  for never more was need.

Go tell thy loving wife said he,
  thy joy and hearts' delight,
That thou must ride miles forty-three
  and shan't come home to night.

Then mind the counsel I shall give,
  and be no whit afraid;
For I can tell you as I live
  your debts will soon be paid.

Mount thy bay nag, and take thy cloak,
  likewise thy morning gown;
And lodge within a hollow oak
  a mile or two from town.

Then you may sleep in sweet content
  all night and take your rest,
And leave it to my management,
  then Sir, a pleasant jest—

Next morning there you shall behold
  the like ne'er seen before;
Which shall produce a sum of gold,
  nay, likewise silver store.

Unto his house straightway he went,
  and told her he must go
A journey, saying be content,
  for why, it must be so.

She seemingly began to weep,
  and with sad sighs reply'd—
You know, alas! I cannot sleep
  without you by my side.

Cries he, kind wife, do not repine,
  why should you sigh and grieve?
I go out to a friend of mine
  some money to receive.

This said, with woman fond deceit,
  she straightway ceas'd to mourn,
And gave him twenty kisses sweet,
  wishing his safe return.

So soon as he was out of sight,
  she for the quaker sent,
And ordered him to come at night,
  that to their heart's content

They may be merry, sport, and play,
  as her husband was from home.
The quaker said, by yea and nay,
  I will not fail to come.

Now just about the close of day
  they did to supper fall;
Now Jack was there as well as they,
  and walk'd about the hall,

And did her fond behaviour note,
  she on her friend did lean,
Jack having his enchanting coat
  was not for to be seen.

Who perfectly did hear and see
  when they did toy and play;
Thought he, I'll be reveng'd on ye,
  before the morning day.

* * * * *

VII.

Jack slays a monstrous giant, and marries a knight's daughter.

Jack Horner a fierce giant kill'd,
  one Galligantus stout,
As large as ever man beheld
  in all the world throughout.

This very giant could with ease,
  step fifteen yards in length:
Up by the root he pluck'd oak trees,
  so mighty was his strength.

His lips did open like two gates,
his beard hung down like wire,
His eyes were like two pewter plates,
he breathed smoke and fire.

'Tis said that he destroy'd as much
as ten score men could eat;
So that the people did him grudge
every bit of meat.

His mess was still continually
two bullocks in a dish;
Then he would drink whole rivers dry,
and thus he starv'd the fish:

He went to drink it seems one day
by a deep river side,
Whereat a lighter fall of straw
did then at anchor ride;

Besides another full of hay;
a third with block and billet;
He cramm'd all these into his maw,
and yet they did not fill it.

He did annoy the nations then,
by night and eke by day;
Whoever passed by his den,
became his fatal pray.

Hard by these liv'd a noble knight,
who had one daughter dear;
For youth and splendid beauty bright
but few could her come near.

He preferr'd her to be the wife,
of him that would destroy,
The bruitish cruel giant's life,
who did them so annoy.

At length Jack Horner being told,
whoever did him slay,
Might have gold and silver eke,
likewise a lady gay;

Quoth Jack, now let me live or die,
  I'll fight this swinging boar;
Though I'm but thirteen inches high,
  and he ten yards and more.

A sword he got five inches long,
  a little cap of steel.
A breast-plate too both stout and strong,
  quoth Jack, I'll make him reel.

Upon a badgers back he got,
  in order to proceed;
Thus being mounted cap-a-pee,
  away he rode full speed.

With double courage stout and bralle,
  he did his valour keep:
Then coming to the giant's cave,
  he found him fast asleep.

His mouth it was not open wide,
  but stood it seems half-cock,
Jack down his throat with speed did ride,
  he never stood to knock.

Jack cut and slash'd his swinging tripes,
  this griev'd the giant sore;
Then did he play upon his pipes,
  which made him dance and roar.

He cry'd, I dance, yet I'm not well,
  there's no man minds my moan:
At length he died and down he fell,
  Then gave a hideous groan.

With that he soon with speed did run,
  and did in brief declare,
What by his valour he had done,
  and gain'd the lady fair.

He marry'd this fair beauty bright,
  her charms he did admire:
And since her father was a knight,
  young Jack became a 'squire.

———

P. 39. l. 11. A couplet is wanting after this line.

P. 39, l. 19. *She whipped them all*, &c. Sometimes this line is thus given:

"She borrow'd a beetle, and she knock'd 'em all o' th' head."

P. 40, l. 18. *Taffy was a Welshman.* Sung on the first of March on the Welsh borders, and other parts of England.

P. 41, l. 9. *Mary had a pretty bird.* This is probably modern.

P. 43, l. 5. *Three blind mice.* The following version is from "Deuteromelia, or the second part of Musicks Melodie, 1609," where the music is also given:

"Three blinde mice, three blinde mice,
Dame Julian, the miller, and his merry old wife,
Shee scrapte her tripe, take thou the knife."

P. 46, l. 7. *Sing a song of sixpence.* It is probable that Sir Toby alludes to this nursery song in "Twelfth Night," act ii. scene 3, when he says, "Come on; there is sixpence for you: let's have a song." The following additional stanza was obtained from the Isle of Man:

"Jenny was so mad,
She didn't know what to do;
She put her finger in her ear,
And crackt it right in two."

P. 48, l. 1. *Little Jenny Wren.* This is part of the tale given at p. 57, and is taken from a farthing merriment.

P. 60, l. 19. *Laughing.* Probably *loffin*, to complete the rhyme. So in "Midsummer Night's Dream," act ii. scene 1:

"And then the whole quire hold their hips, and loffe."

P. 61, l. 1. *She took a clean dish.* Sometimes thus:

"She went to the triper's."

P. 63, l. 1. *Old King Cole.* This ought to have been placed in the first class. It is a singular fact that *King Cole* was one of the ancient British kings. The following two versions differ from that which I have printed in the text:

I.

"Old King Coel
Was a merry old soul,
And a merry old soul was he;
Old King Coel,
He sat in his hole,
And he call'd for his *fiddlers three*, &c.

"The first, he was an Irishman;
The second, he was a Scot;
The third, he was a Welshman;
And all were rogues, I wot.

"The Irishman lov'd usquebaugh;
The Scot was drown'd in ale;
The Welshman had like to be chok'd by a mouse,
But he pull'd her out by the tail."

II.

"Old King Coel
Was a merry old soul,
And a merry old soul was he;
Old King Coel,
He sat in his hole,
And he call'd for his *pipers three*.

"The first, he was a miller;
The second, he was a weaver;
The third, he was a tailor;
And all were rogues together.

"The miller, he stole corn;
The weaver, he stole yarn;
The little tailor stole broad-cloth,
To keep these three rogues warm.

"The miller was drown'd in his dam;
The weaver was hung in his loom;
And the devil ran away with the little tailor,
With the broad-cloth under his arm."

P. 64, l. 17. *There was a lady all skin and bone.* The following version was obtained from Yorkshire, where it is used in a nursery game:

"There was an old woman she went to church to pray;
And when she got to the church-yard stile,
She sat her down to think a little while;
And when she got to the church-yard door,
She sat her down, to think a little more;
And when she got the church within,
She knelt her down to pray for sin;
She look'd above, she look'd below,
She saw a dead man lying low;
The worms crept in, and the worms crept out;
She ask'd the parson, 'may I go out?'
Yes, you may," &c.

P. 70, l. 7. *There was a frog liv'd in a well.* The tune to this is given in a scarce work, called "The Merry Musician, or a Cure for the Spleen," 12mo., and also in "An Antidote to Melancholy," 1719. The well-known song, "A frog he would a wooing go," appears to have been borrowed from this. See Dauney's "Ancient Scottish Melodies," p. 53.

P. 72, l. 12. *There was an old woman.* Sung to the air of *Liliburlero.* See "Musick's Handmaid," 1673, where the air is called, "Liliburlero, or Old Woman whither so high."

P. 79, l. 10. *Ding, dong, bell.* The burden to a song in the "Tempest," act i. scene 2; and also to one in the "Merchant of Venice."

P. 80, l. 2. *Dog with long snout.* Sometimes, "Little Johnny Grout."

P. 84, l. 5. Another version runs thus:

> "Give a thing,
> Take a thing,
> That's the devil's golden ring."

P. 86, No. 124. A game.

P. 87, l. 9. *Tommy Tibule.* A game on a child's toes.

P. 90, l. 5. *Ride to the market.* A game on the nurse's knee.

P. 100, l. 1. *Bisiter.* That is, Bicester, in Oxfordshire.

P. 103, l. 19. *Was.* Probably "wasn't."

P. 104, l. 3. This is said to have been written by Dr. Wallis.

P. 105, l. 14. The charm in the *Townley Mysteries*, to which I refer, is as follows:

> "For ferde we be fryght a crosse let us kest,
> Cryst crosse, benedyght, eest and west,
> For dreede.
> Jesus o' Nazorus,
> Crucyefixus,
> Marcus, Andreas,
> God be our spede."

P. 106, l. 5. The two last lines of this charm are perhaps imitated from the following in Bishop Ken's *Evening Hymn:*

> "Let my blest guardian, while I sleep,
> His watchful station near me keep."

P. 107, l. 1. *We are three brethren.* Sometimes "knights." The versions of this game vary considerably from each other.

P. 109, l. 1. *Girls and boys.* The tune to this may be found in all the late editions of Playford's "Dancing Master."

P 112, No. 194. The following is a Scotch version of this game:

"1. Buff says Buff to all his men.
2. I say Buff to you again.
1. Methinks Buff smiles.
2. No, Buff never smiles,
But strokes his face
With a very good grace,
And passes the staff to another."

P. 116, l. 1. A game on a slate.

P. 113, l. 17. *Queen Anne.* A different version of No. 184, p. 108.

P. 114, l. 15. *Then comes.* Sometimes, "Then comes down."

P. 117, l. 6. *Eleven comets in the sky.* This ought to be said in one breath. The following is another version of it:

"Eight ships on the main,
I wish them all safe back again;
Seven eagles in the air,
I wonder how they all came there;
I don't know, nor I don't care.
Six spiders on the wall,
Close to an old woman's apple-stall;
Five puppies in Highgate Hall,
Who daily for their breakfast call;
Four mares stuck in a bog;
Three monkies tied to a log;
Two pudding-ends will choke a dog,
With a gaping, wide-mouthed, waddling frog."

P. 133, l. 5. *The rule of the road.* I am told that this is a very modern composition.

P. 131, l. 1. For "dee," read "D."

P. 131, l. 3, No. 123. See page 124.

P. 133, l. 4. *E. with a figure fiftie.* This ought to be thus:

"E. with a figure of L. fiftie."

This is probably an epigram on one of the family of the Noels, or Nowels.

P. 134, l. 9. *Cowslips.* Some read "muscles." I have a copy of the date 1797, which has "cuckolds," probably the genuine old reading.

P. 137, No. 251. *When I was a little girl.* A friend has kindly furnished me with a different version of these curious lines:

"When I was a little girl,
I wash'd my mammy's dishes:
I put my finger in my eye,
And pull'd out four-score fishes.

"My mammy call'd me good girl,
And bade me do so 'gain:
I put my finger in my eye,
And pull'd out fourscore-ten."

It is a singular fact, that a comparatively modern discovery in physiology was anticipated in the original version of this song.

P. 142, No. 263. This is a game.

P. 144, l. 1. *We'll go a shooting.* This is an English version of a very curious song, used on the occasion of "hunting the wran," on St. Stephen's Day, in the Isle of Man. On that day the children of the villagers procure a wren, attach it with a string to a branch of holly, decorate the branch with pieces of ribbon that they beg from the various houses, and carry it through the village, singing these lines. An extract from an Irish work, from which it appears that this custom is likewise prevalent in Ireland, is given in Sir Henry Ellis's edition of Brand's "Popular Antiquities," vol. ii. p. 516:— "The Druids represented this as the king of all birds. The great respect shown to this bird gave great offence to the first Christian missionaries, and, by their command, he is still hunted and killed by the peasants on Christmas Day, and on the following (St. Stephen's Day) he is carried about hung by the leg in the centre of two hoops, crossing each other at right angles, and a procession made in every village, of men, women, and children, importing him to be the king of birds." I am glad to be able to give the genuine traditional song, as recited in the Isle of Man:

THE HUNTING OF THE WRAN.

"We'll hunt the wran, says Robin to Bobbin;
We'll hunt the wran, says Richard to Robin;
We'll hunt the wran, says Jack o' th' land;
We'll hunt the wran, says every one.

"Where shall we find him? says Robin to Bobbin;
Where shall we find him? says Richard to Robin;
Where shall we find him? says Jack o' th' land;
Where shall we find him? says every one.

"In yon green bush, says Robin to Bobbin;
In yon green bush, says Richard to Robin;
In yon green bush, says Jack o' th' land;
In yon green bush, says every one.

"How shall we kill him? says Robin to Bobbin;
How shall we kill him? says Richard to Robin;
How shall we kill him? says Jack o' th' land;
How shall we kill him? says every one.

"With sticks and stones, says Robin to Bobbin;
With sticks and stones, says Richard to Robin;
With sticks and stones, says Jack o' th' land;
With sticks and stones, says every one.

"How shall we get him home? says Robin to Bobbin;
How shall we get him home? says Richard to Robin;
How shall we get him home? says Jack o' th' land;
How shall we get him home? says every one.

"We'll borrow a cart, says Robin to Bobbin;
We'll borrow a cart, says Richard to Robin;
We'll borrow a cart, says Jack o' th' land;
We'll borrow a cart, says every one.

"How shall we boil him? says Robin to Bobbin;
How shall we boil him? says Richard to Robin;
How shall we boil him? says Jack o' th' land;
How shall we boil him? says every one.

"In the brewery pan, says Robin to Bobbin;
In the brewery pan, says Richard to Robin;
In the brewery pan, says Jack o' th' land;
In the brewery pan, says every one."

In the copy which was given to me, there were two additional stanzas, beginning respectively, "How shall we eat him?" and, "With knives and forks:" but these are probably modern interpolations.

P. 149, No. 297. There is another couplet on this sovereign, which runs thus,—

"Thomas a Didymus had a black beard,
Kiss'd Nancy Fitchett, and made her afeard."

P. 149, No. 282. *Bobby Shaft.* This ought to be, "Bobby Shaftoe," a member of a celebrated family at the end of the seventeenth century.

P. 151, l. 17. *Of all the gay birds.* These four lines are part of an old song, the whole of which may be found in "Deuteromelia," 4to. Lond. 1609, and it is singular that it should have come down to us from oral tradition. This version was obtained from Lincolnshire. The following copy is taken from the work here quoted: but there are considerable variations in later copies, some of which may be more correct.

"Of all the birds that ever I see,
The owle is the fayrest in her degree:
For all the day long she sits in a tree,
And when the night comes, away flies she!
Te whit, te whow!
Sir knave to thou,
This song is well sung, I make you a vow,
And he is a knave that drinketh now.
Nose, nose, nose, nose!
And who gave you that jolly red nose?
Sinamont, and ginger, nutmegs and cloves,—
And that gave me my jolly red nose!"

INDEX.

Lightning Source UK Ltd.
Milton Keynes UK
UKOW04f1557081216
289394UK00001B/117/P

9 781278 428000